Photoshop® 6

– In an Instant –

by Michael Toot and Mike Wooldridge

Visual

From
maranGraphics®

&

Hungry Minds™

Best-Selling Books • Digital Downloads • e-Books • Answer Networks
e-Newsletters • Branded Web Sites • e-Learning

New York, NY • Cleveland, OH • Indianapolis, IN

Photoshop® 6 In an Instant

Published by
Hungry Minds, Inc.
909 Third Avenue
New York, NY 10022
www.hungryminds.com

maranGraphics, Inc.
5755 Coopers Avenue
Mississauga, Ontario, Canada
L4Z 1R9
Library of Congress Control Number: 2001091949
ISBN: 0-7645-3629-X
Printed in the United States of America
10 9 8 7 6 5 4 3 2 1
1B/TR/QX/QR/IN
Distributed in the United States by Hungry Minds, Inc.
Distributed by CDG Books Canada Inc. for Canada; by Transworld Publishers Limited in the United Kingdom; by IDG Norge Books for Norway; by IDG Sweden Books for Sweden; by IDG Books Australia Publishing Corporation Pty. Ltd. for Australia and New Zealand; by TransQuest Publishers Pte Ltd. for Singapore, Malaysia, Thailand, Indonesia, and Hong Kong; by Gotop Information Inc. for Taiwan; by ICG Muse, Inc. for Japan; by Intersoft for South Africa; by Eyrolles for France; by International Thomson Publishing for Germany, Austria, and Switzerland; by Distribuidora Cuspide for Argentina; by LR International for Brazil; by Galileo Libros for Chile; by Ediciones ZETA S.C.R. Ltda. for Peru; by WS Computer Publishing Corporation, Inc., for the Philippines; by Contemporanea de Ediciones for Venezuela; by Express Computer Distributors for the Caribbean and West Indies; by Micronesia Media Distributor, Inc., for Micronesia; by Chips Computadoras S.A. de C.V. for Mexico; by Editorial Norma de Panama S.A. for Panama; by American Bookshops for Finland.
For corporate orders, please call maranGraphics at 800-469-6616 or fax 905-890-9434.
For general information on Hungry Minds' products and services, please contact our Customer Care Department within the U.S. at 800-762-2974, outside the U.S. at 317-572-3993, or fax 317-572-4002.
For sales inquiries and reseller information, including discounts, premium and bulk quantity sales, and foreign-language translations, please contact our Customer Care Department at 800-434-3422, fax 317-572-4002, or write to Hungry Minds, Inc., Attn: Customer Care Department, 10475 Crosspoint Boulevard, Indianapolis, IN 46256.
For information on licensing foreign or domestic rights, please contact our Sub-Rights Customer Care Department at 212-884-5000.
For information on using Hungry Minds' products and services in the classroom or for ordering examination copies, please contact our Educational Sales Department at 800-434-2086 or fax 317-572-4005.
For press review copies, author interviews, or other publicity information, please contact our Public Relations department at 317-572-3168 or fax 317-572-4168.
For authorization to photocopy items for corporate, personal, or educational use, please contact Copyright Clearance Center, 222 Rosewood Drive, Danvers, MA 01923, or fax 978-750-4470.
Screen shots displayed in this book are based on pre-released software and are subject to change.

Trademark Acknowledgments

Permissions

is a trademark of Hungry Minds, Inc.

Hungry Minds™

U.S. Corporate Sales	U.S. Trade Sales
Contact maranGraphics at (800) 469-6616 or fax (905) 890-9434.	Contact Hungry Minds at (800) 434-3422 or fax (317) 572-4002.

Some comments from our readers...

"I have to praise you and your company on the fine products you turn out. I have twelve of the *Teach Yourself VISUALLY* and *Simplified* books in my house. They were instrumental in helping me pass a difficult computer course. Thank you for creating books that are easy to follow."

—*Gordon Justin (Brielle, NJ)*

"I commend your efforts and your success. I teach in an outreach program for the Dr. Eugene Clark Library in Lockhart, TX. Your *Teach Yourself VISUALLY* books are incredible and I use them in my computer classes. All my students love them!"

—*Michele Schalin (Lockhart, TX)*

"Thank you so much for helping people like me learn about computers. The Maran family is just what the doctor ordered. Thank you, thank you, thank you."

—*Carol Moten (New Kensington, PA)*

"I would like to take this time to compliment maranGraphics on creating such great books. Thank you for making it clear. Keep up the good work."

—*Kirk Santoro (Burbank, CA)*

"I write to extend my thanks and appreciation for your books. They are clear, easy to follow, and straight to the point. Keep up the good work!"

—*Seward Kollie (Dakar, Senegal)*

"What fantastic teaching books you have produced! Congratulations to you and your staff. You deserve the Nobel prize in Education in the Software category. Thanks for helping me to understand computers."

—*Bruno Tonon (Melbourne, Australia)*

"Over time, I have bought a number of your 'Read Less - Learn More' books. For me, they are THE way to learn anything easily."

—*José A. Mazón (Cuba, NY)*

"I was introduced to maranGraphics about four years ago and YOU ARE THE GREATEST THING THAT EVER HAPPENED TO INTRODUCTORY COMPUTER BOOKS!"

—*Glenn Nettleton (Huntsville, AL)*

"Compliments To The Chef!! Your books are extraordinary! Or, simply put, Extra-Ordinary, meaning way above the rest! THANK YOU THANK YOU THANK YOU! for creating these."

—*Christine J. Manfrin (Castle Rock, CO)*

"I'm a grandma who was pushed by an 11-year-old grandson to join the computer age. I found myself hopelessly confused and frustrated until I discovered the Visual series. I'm no expert by any means now, but I'm a lot further along than I would have been otherwise. Thank you!"

—*Carol Louthain (Logansport, IN)*

"Thank you, thank you, thank you...for making it so easy for me to break into this high-tech world. I now own four of your books. I recommend them to anyone who is a beginner like myself. Now... if you could just do one for programming VCRs, it would make my day!"

—*Gay O'Donnell (Calgary, Alberta, Canada)*

"You're marvelous! I am greatly in your debt."

—*Patrick Baird (Lacey, WA)*

maranGraphics is a family-run business located near Toronto, Canada.

At maranGraphics, we believe in producing great computer books – one book at a time.

Each maranGraphics book uses the award-winning communication process that we have been developing over the last 25 years. Using this process, we organize screen shots and text in a way that makes it easy for you to learn new concepts and tasks.

We spend hours deciding the best way to perform each task, so you don't have to!

Our clear, easy-to-follow screen shots and instructions walk you through each task from beginning to end.

We want to thank you for purchasing what we feel are the best computer books money can buy. We hope you enjoy using this book as much as we enjoyed creating it!

Sincerely,

The Maran Family

Please visit us on the Web at:

www.maran.com

TABLE OF CONTENTS

TABLE OF CONTENTS

SET PHOTOSHOP PREFERENCES

Photoshop's Preferences dialog boxes enable you to change default settings and customize how the program looks.

SET PHOTOSHOP PREFERENCES

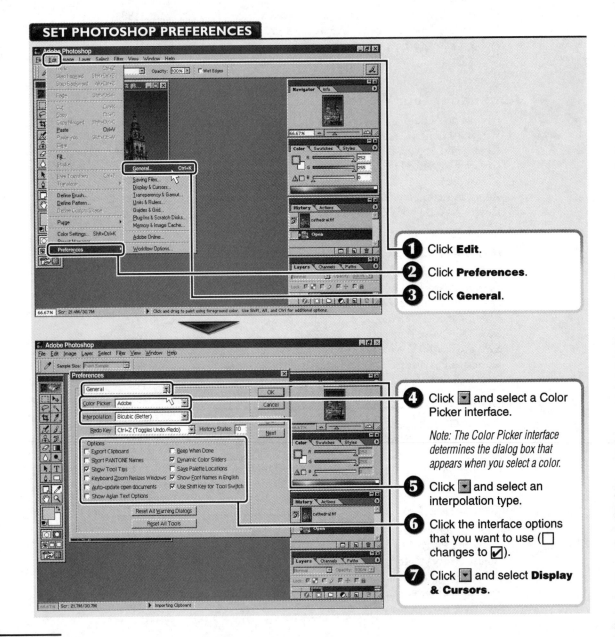

1 Click **Edit**.

2 Click **Preferences**.

3 Click **General**.

4 Click ▾ and select a Color Picker interface.

Note: The Color Picker interface determines the dialog box that appears when you select a color.

5 Click ▾ and select an interpolation type.

6 Click the interface options that you want to use (☐ changes to ☑).

7 Click ▾ and select **Display & Cursors**.

in an *instant*

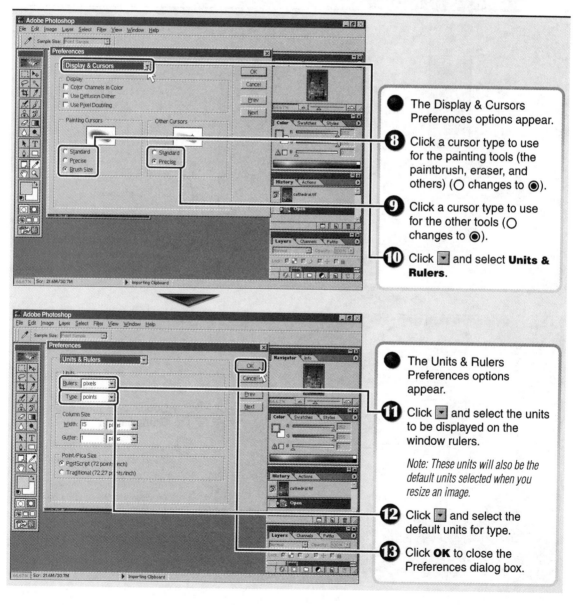

The Display & Cursors
Preferences options appear.

8 Click a cursor type to use
for the painting tools (the
paintbrush, eraser, and
others) (○ changes to ◉).

9 Click a cursor type to use
for the other tools (○
changes to ◉).

10 Click ▼ and select **Units &
Rulers**.

The Units & Rulers
Preferences options
appear.

11 Click ▼ and select the units
to be displayed on the
window rulers.

*Note: These units will also be the
default units selected when you
resize an image.*

12 Click ▼ and select the
default units for type.

13 Click **OK** to close the
Preferences dialog box.

CALIBRATE YOUR MONITOR

You can calibrate your monitor to ensure that colors display accurately and reliably when you use Photoshop.

CALIBRATE YOUR MONITOR

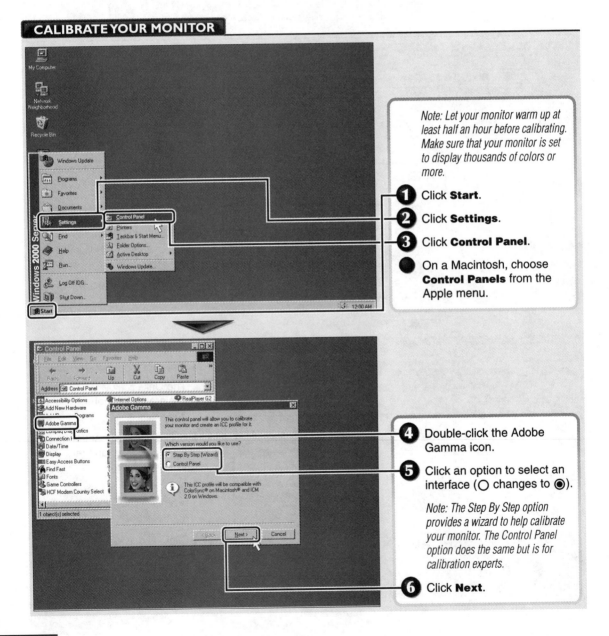

Note: Let your monitor warm up at least half an hour before calibrating. Make sure that your monitor is set to display thousands of colors or more.

1 Click **Start**.

2 Click **Settings**.

3 Click **Control Panel**.

● On a Macintosh, choose **Control Panels** from the Apple menu.

4 Double-click the Adobe Gamma icon.

5 Click an option to select an interface (○ changes to ◉).

Note: The Step By Step option provides a wizard to help calibrate your monitor. The Control Panel option does the same but is for calibration experts.

6 Click **Next**.

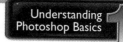
in an *instant*

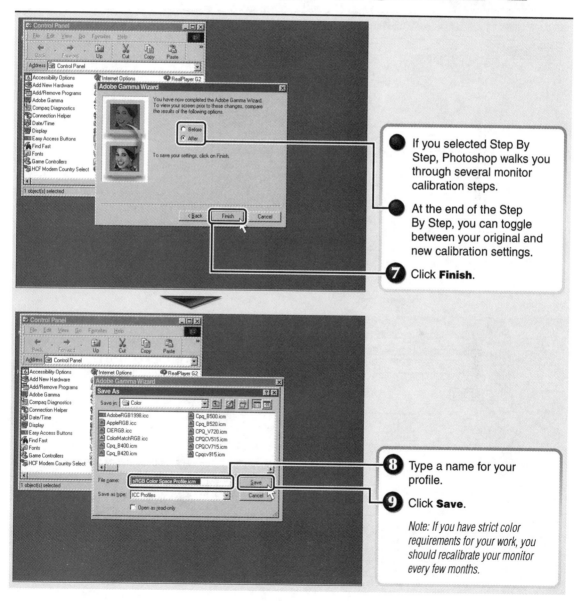

● If you selected Step By
Step, Photoshop walks you
through several monitor
calibration steps.

● At the end of the Step
By Step, you can toggle
between your original and
new calibration settings.

7 Click **Finish**.

8 Type a name for your
profile.

9 Click **Save**.

*Note: If you have strict color
requirements for your work, you
should recalibrate your monitor
every few months.*

OPEN AN IMAGE

You can open an existing image file in Photoshop.

OPEN AN IMAGE

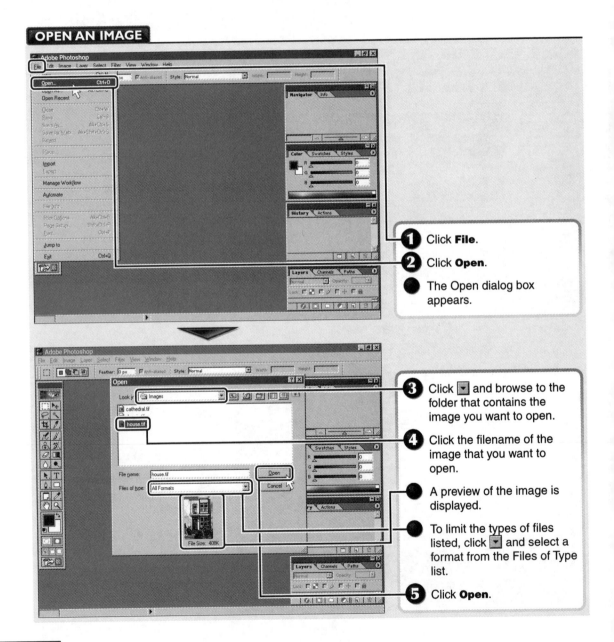

1 Click **File**.

2 Click **Open**.

● The Open dialog box appears.

3 Click ▼ and browse to the folder that contains the image you want to open.

4 Click the filename of the image that you want to open.

● A preview of the image is displayed.

● To limit the types of files listed, click ▼ and select a format from the Files of Type list.

5 Click **Open**.

in an *instant*

● Photoshop opens the image in a new window.

● The filename appears in the title bar.

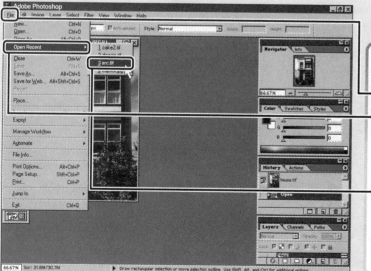

OPEN RECENTLY ACCESSED IMAGES

① Click **File**.

② Click **Open Recent**.

● Photoshop displays a list of files that you recently worked on.

③ Click the filename of the image that you want to open.

● Photoshop opens the image in a new window.

CREATE A NEW IMAGE

You can start a Photoshop project by creating a blank image.

CREATE A NEW IMAGE

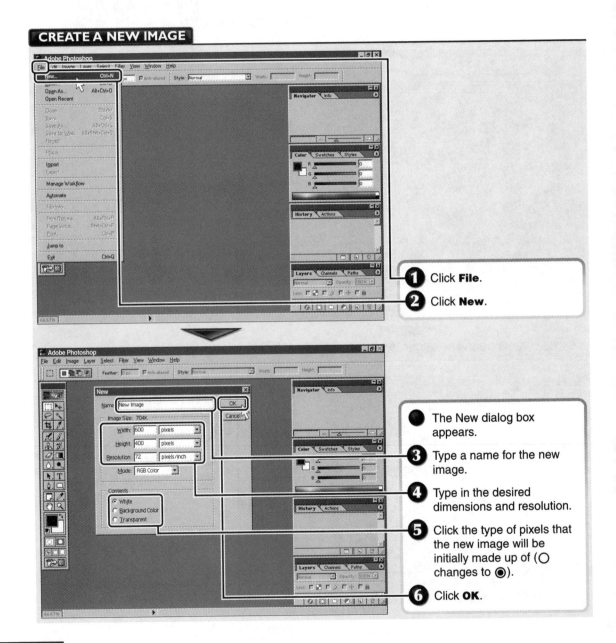

1 Click **File**.

2 Click **New**.

● The New dialog box appears.

3 Type a name for the new image.

4 Type in the desired dimensions and resolution.

5 Click the type of pixels that the new image will be initially made up of (○ changes to ◉).

6 Click **OK**.

in an *instant*

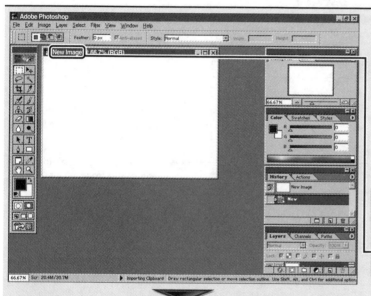

● Photoshop creates a new image window at the specified dimensions.

● The filename appears in the title bar.

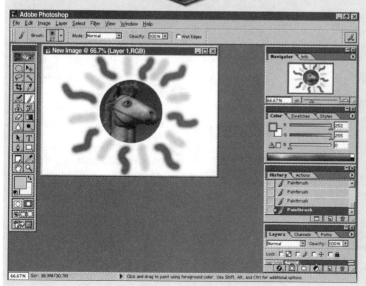

7 Use Photoshop's tools and commands to create your image.

● In this example, part of another image has been cut and pasted into the window, and color streaks were added with the Paintbrush tool.

Note: To find out how to save your image, see Chapter 13.

EXECUTE PHOTOSHOP COMMANDS

You can make changes to an image by executing
a Photoshop command. You can undo your changes,
if necessary, by using the Undo command.

EXECUTE PHOTOSHOP COMMANDS

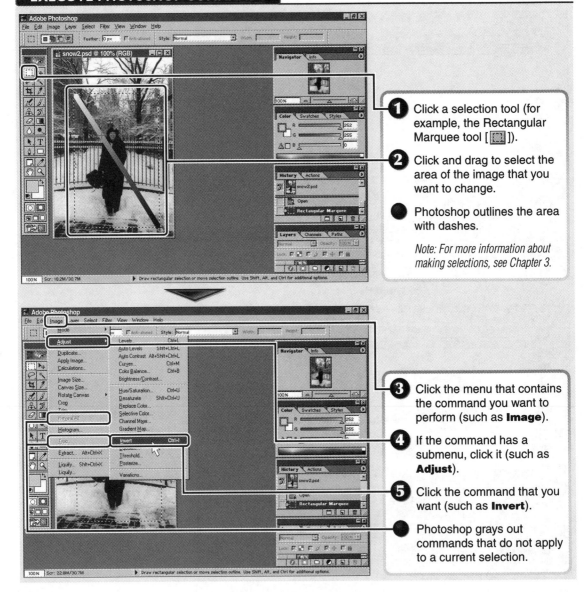

1 Click a selection tool (for
example, the Rectangular
Marquee tool [▭]).

2 Click and drag to select the
area of the image that you
want to change.

● Photoshop outlines the area
with dashes.

*Note: For more information about
making selections, see Chapter 3.*

3 Click the menu that contains
the command you want to
perform (such as **Image**).

4 If the command has a
submenu, click it (such as
Adjust).

5 Click the command that you
want (such as **Invert**).

● Photoshop grays out
commands that do not apply
to a current selection.

in an *instant*

● Photoshop applies the command to the selected area in the image.

Note: If you do not make a selection before executing a command, Photoshop applies the command to the entire image (or selected layer, depending on the command).

UNDO A COMMAND

1 Click **Edit**.

2 Click **Undo**.

● The selection returns to its original state.

Note: You can use the History palette to undo multiple commands (see the section "Undo Commands or Revert to the Last Saved State").

Note: You can also press **Ctrl** + **Z** *(⌘ + Z) to undo a command.*

MAGNIFY IMAGES AND DETAILS

You can change the magnification of
an image with the Zoom tool.

MAGNIFY IMAGES AND DETAILS

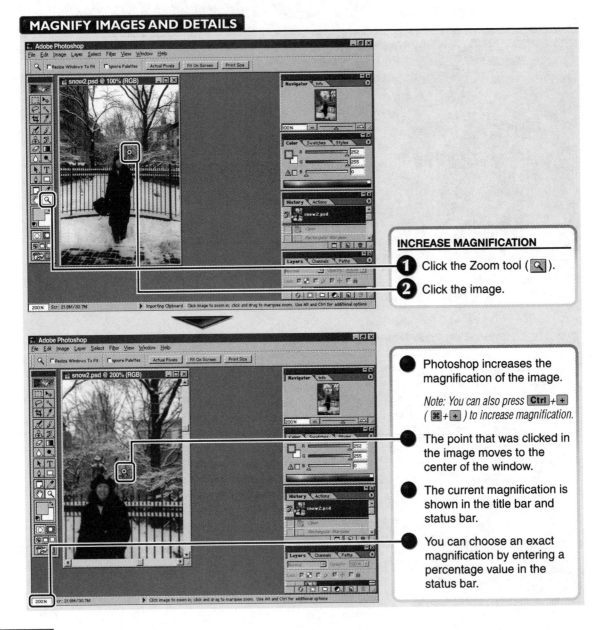

INCREASE MAGNIFICATION

1 Click the Zoom tool ( ).

2 Click the image.

● Photoshop increases the
magnification of the image.

Note: You can also press Ctrl + +
(⌘ + + *) to increase magnification.*

● The point that was clicked in
the image moves to the
center of the window.

● The current magnification is
shown in the title bar and
status bar.

● You can choose an exact
magnification by entering a
percentage value in the
status bar.

in an *instant*

DECREASE MAGNIFICATION

1 With 🔍 selected, press and hold **Alt** (**option**) and click the image.

⬤ The original image was clicked to reduce the magnification to 66.7%.

Note: You can also press **Ctrl** + **–** (**⌘** + **–**) *to decrease magnification.*

MAGNIFY A DETAIL

1 Click and drag with 🔍 to select the detail.

⬤ The object appears enlarged on-screen.

ADJUST IMAGE VIEWS

You can move an image within the window by using the Hand tool or by using the scroll bars.

ADJUST IMAGE VIEWS

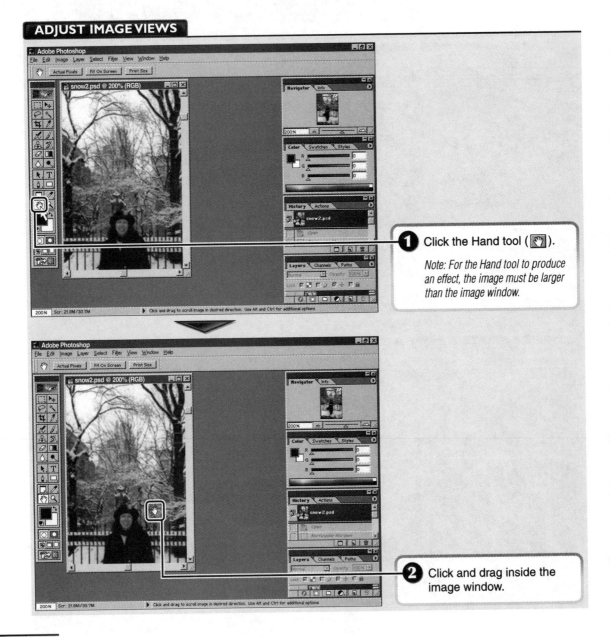

1 Click the Hand tool ( ).

Note: For the Hand tool to produce an effect, the image must be larger than the image window.

2 Click and drag inside the image window.

in an instant

The view of the image shifts inside the window.

Note: The Hand tool is a more flexible alternative to using the scroll bars.

3 Click and hold the window's scroll bar button.

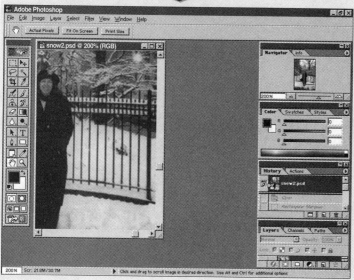

The image scrolls horizontally.

Note: Unlike the scroll bars, the Hand tool enables you to move the image freely in two dimensions.

CHANGE SCREEN MODES

You can switch the screen mode to change the look of your work space on-screen.

CHANGE SCREEN MODES

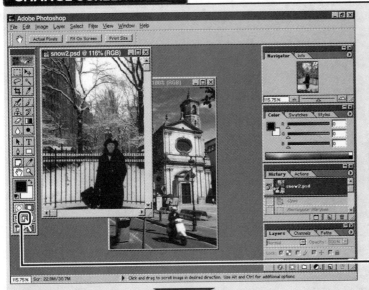

SWITCH TO FULL SCREEN MODE WITH MENU BAR

Note: The standard screen mode enables you to view multiple images at once, each in a different window.

1 Click ▣.

● Photoshop puts the current image window in the center of a blank, full-screen canvas with the menu options at the top of the screen.

in an *instant*

SWITCH TO FULL SCREEN MODE

1 Click ☐.

● The image appears full screen without the menu.

CLOSE TOOLBOX AND PALETTES

1 Press **Tab**.

● Photoshop closes all toolboxes and palettes.

*Note: The **Tab** feature works in all of Photoshop's screen modes.*

*Note: To view the toolbox and palettes, you can press **Tab** again.*

VIEW RULERS AND GUIDES

You can turn on rulers and create guides, which help you accurately place elements in your image.

VIEW RULERS AND GUIDES

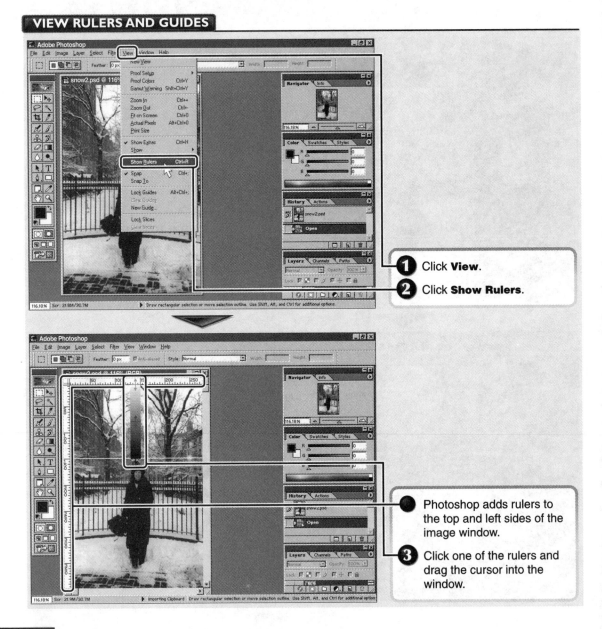

1 Click **View**.

2 Click **Show Rulers**.

● Photoshop adds rulers to the top and left sides of the image window.

3 Click one of the rulers and drag the cursor into the window.

in an *instant*

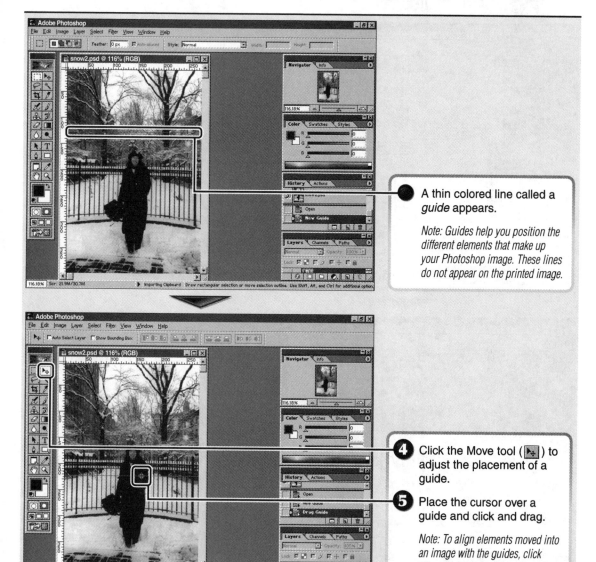

A thin colored line called a *guide* appears.

Note: Guides help you position the different elements that make up your Photoshop image. These lines do not appear on the printed image.

④ Click the Move tool (📬) to adjust the placement of a guide.

⑤ Place the cursor over a guide and click and drag.

Note: To align elements moved into an image with the guides, click **View**, **Snap To**, *and then* **Guides**.

You can turn on a grid that overlays your image. The grid is similar to a set of guides (see the section "View Rulers and Guides") and helps you organize elements within your image. The grid provides a quick way to align images neatly throughout your project.

VIEW A GRID

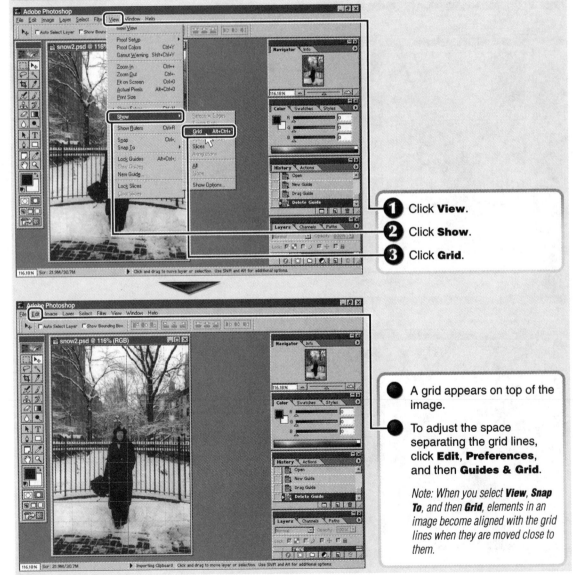

1 Click **View**.

2 Click **Show**.

3 Click **Grid**.

● A grid appears on top of the image.

● To adjust the space separating the grid lines, click **Edit**, **Preferences**, and then **Guides & Grid**.

*Note: When you select **View**, **Snap To**, and then **Grid**, elements in an image become aligned with the grid lines when they are moved close to them.*

USING SHORTCUTS TO SELECT TOOLS

You can press letter keys to select items in the toolbox. This can sometimes be more efficient than clicking the tools.

USING SHORTCUTS TO SELECT TOOLS

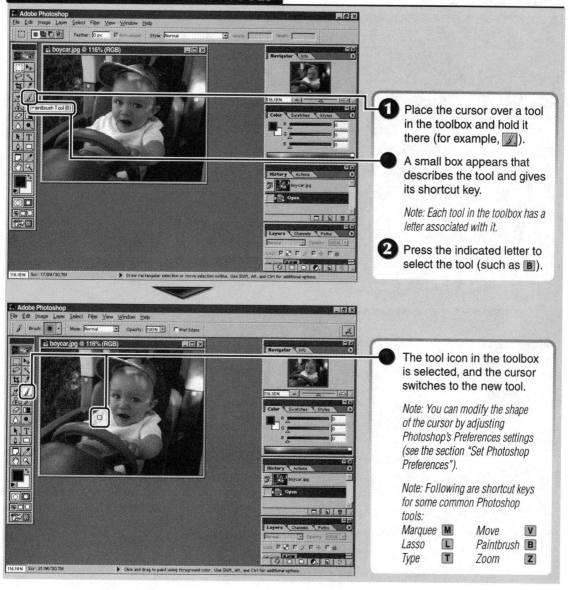

1. Place the cursor over a tool in the toolbox and hold it there (for example, ✍).

   A small box appears that describes the tool and gives its shortcut key.

   Note: Each tool in the toolbox has a letter associated with it.

2. Press the indicated letter to select the tool (such as B).

   The tool icon in the toolbox is selected, and the cursor switches to the new tool.

   Note: You can modify the shape of the cursor by adjusting Photoshop's Preferences settings (see the section "Set Photoshop Preferences").

   Note: Following are shortcut keys for some common Photoshop tools:

Marquee	M	Move	V
Lasso	L	Paintbrush	B
Type	T	Zoom	Z

UNDO COMMANDS OR REVERT TO THE LAST SAVED STATE

You can undo multiple commands or revert to a previously saved state by using the History palette.

UNDO COMMANDS

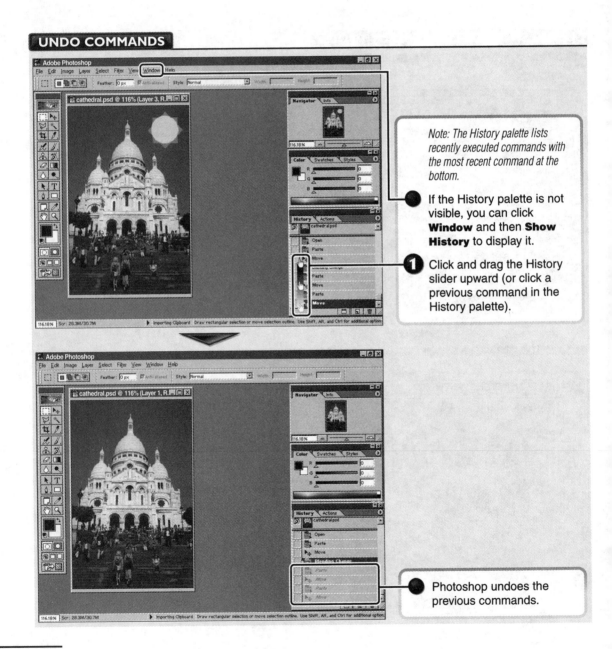

Note: The History palette lists recently executed commands with the most recent command at the bottom.

■ If the History palette is not visible, you can click **Window** and then **Show History** to display it.

① Click and drag the History slider upward (or click a previous command in the History palette).

■ Photoshop undoes the previous commands.

in an *instant*

REVERT TO THE LAST SAVED STATE

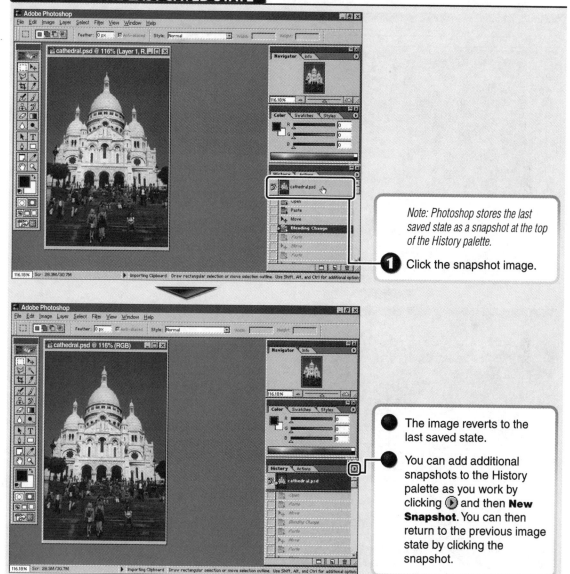

Note: Photoshop stores the last saved state as a snapshot at the top of the History palette.

1 Click the snapshot image.

● The image reverts to the last saved state.

● You can add additional snapshots to the History palette as you work by clicking ▶ and then **New Snapshot**. You can then return to the previous image state by clicking the snapshot.

CHANGE AN IMAGE'S ON-SCREEN SIZE

You can change the size at which an image is displayed on your computer monitor so that you can see the entire image.

CHANGE AN IMAGE'S ON-SCREEN SIZE

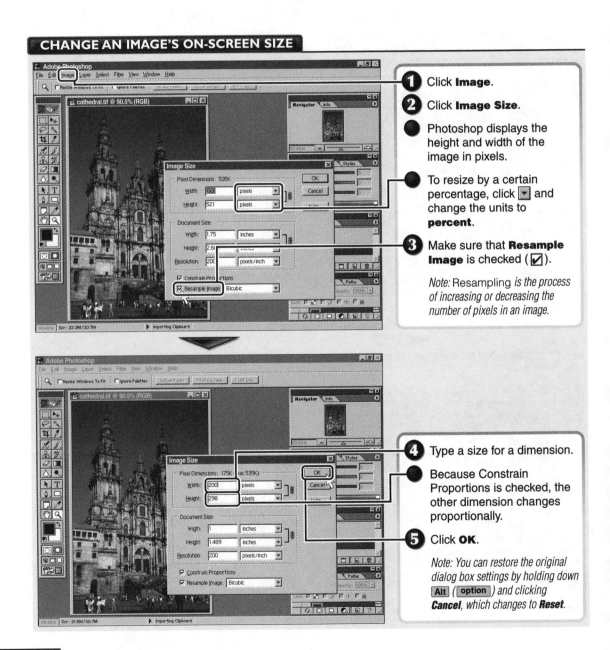

1 Click **Image**.

2 Click **Image Size**.

● Photoshop displays the height and width of the image in pixels.

● To resize by a certain percentage, click ▼ and change the units to **percent**.

3 Make sure that **Resample Image** is checked (☑).

Note: Resampling is the process of increasing or decreasing the number of pixels in an image.

4 Type a size for a dimension.

● Because Constrain Proportions is checked, the other dimension changes proportionally.

5 Click **OK**.

Note: You can restore the original dialog box settings by holding down **Alt** *(* **option** *) and clicking* **Cancel***, which changes to* **Reset***.*

in an *instant*

● Photoshop resizes the image.

Note: Changing the number of pixels in an image can add blur. To sharpen a resized image, apply the Unsharp Mask filter (see Chapter 10).

Note: You lose less detail when you decrease an image's size than when you increase it. You are better off starting with an image that is too big than one that is too small.

● This image was resized by setting the units to **percent** and typing **25** in the Width and Height fields. Photoshop decreased the image dimensions by three quarters.

CHANGE AN IMAGE'S PRINT SIZE

You can change the printed size of an image.
This gives you the flexibility of fitting an image
onto a single print page for viewing.

CHANGE AN IMAGE'S PRINT SIZE

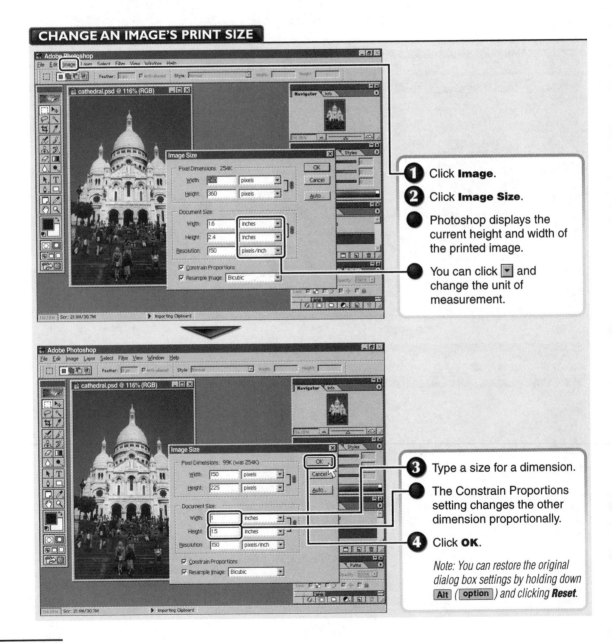

1 Click **Image**.

2 Click **Image Size**.

Photoshop displays the
current height and width of
the printed image.

You can click ▼ and
change the unit of
measurement.

3 Type a size for a dimension.

The Constrain Proportions
setting changes the other
dimension proportionally.

4 Click **OK**.

*Note: You can restore the original
dialog box settings by holding down
Alt (option) and clicking Reset.*

in an instant

● Photoshop resizes the image.

Note: Changing the number of pixels in an image can add blur. To sharpen a resized image, apply the Unsharp Mask filter (see Chapter 10).

● This image was resized with Constrain Proportions unchecked and the width changed. Photoshop decreases the width but not the height.

You can change the print resolution of an image to increase or decrease the print quality.

CHANGE AN IMAGE'S PRINT RESOLUTION

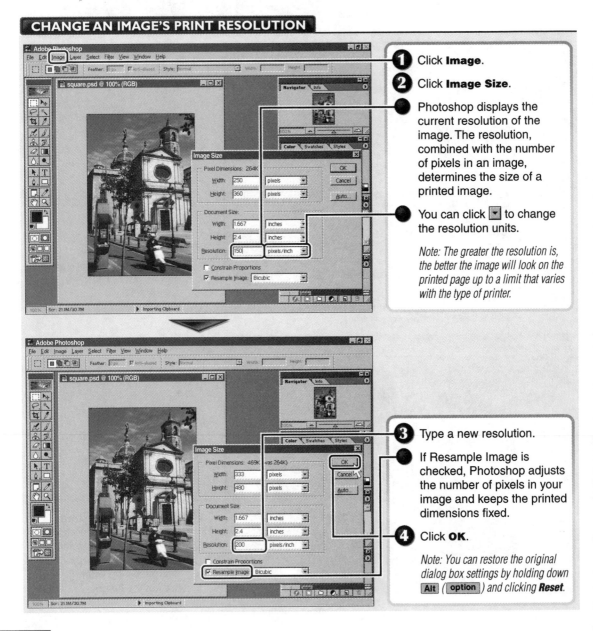

1 Click **Image**.

2 Click **Image Size**.

Photoshop displays the current resolution of the image. The resolution, combined with the number of pixels in an image, determines the size of a printed image.

You can click ▼ to change the resolution units.

Note: The greater the resolution is, the better the image will look on the printed page up to a limit that varies with the type of printer.

3 Type a new resolution.

If Resample Image is checked, Photoshop adjusts the number of pixels in your image and keeps the printed dimensions fixed.

4 Click **OK**.

Note: You can restore the original dialog box settings by holding down **Alt** *(* **option** *) and clicking **Reset**.*

in an instant

Modifying the resolution has changed the number of pixels in the image, so the on-screen image changes in size. (The print size stays the same.)

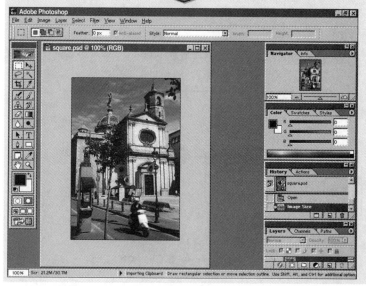

The resolution of this image was increased with resampling turned off. The on-screen image stays the same size. The printed size will be smaller.

The image canvas is the area on which an image sits. You can change the canvas size of an image to adjust its rectangular shape or to add blank space to its sides.

CHANGE AN IMAGE'S CANVAS SIZE

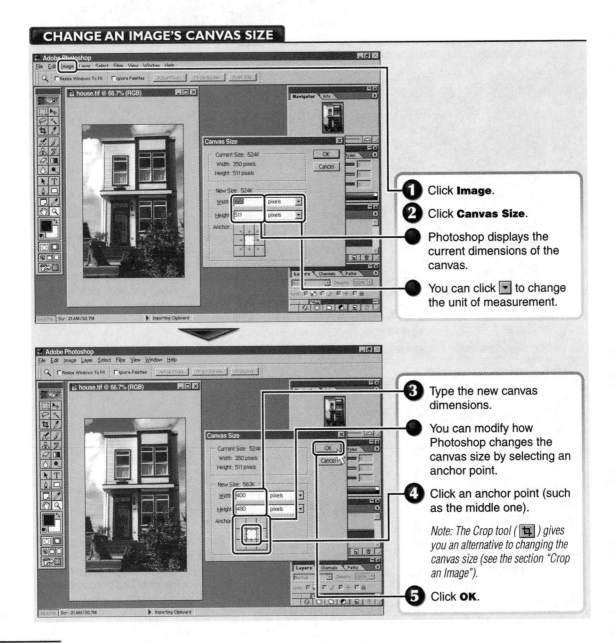

1 Click **Image**.

2 Click **Canvas Size**.

Photoshop displays the current dimensions of the canvas.

You can click ▼ to change the unit of measurement.

3 Type the new canvas dimensions.

You can modify how Photoshop changes the canvas size by selecting an anchor point.

4 Click an anchor point (such as the middle one).

Note: The Crop tool (⛏) gives you an alternative to changing the canvas size (see the section "Crop an Image").

5 Click **OK**.

in an *instant*

- If you decrease a dimension, Photoshop displays a dialog box asking whether you want to proceed. Click **Proceed**.

- Photoshop changes the image's canvas size.

- Because the middle anchor point was selected in this example, the canvas size changes equally on all sides.

- Photoshop fills any new canvas space with the background color (in this case, white).

- This canvas was resized by the same dimensions as the previous example, but with the lower-left anchor point selected.

- The canvas width changes only on the right side; the canvas height changes only on the top.

CROP AN IMAGE

You can use the Crop tool to trim off parts of an image that you do not want or to balance the image better within the canvas.

CROP AN IMAGE

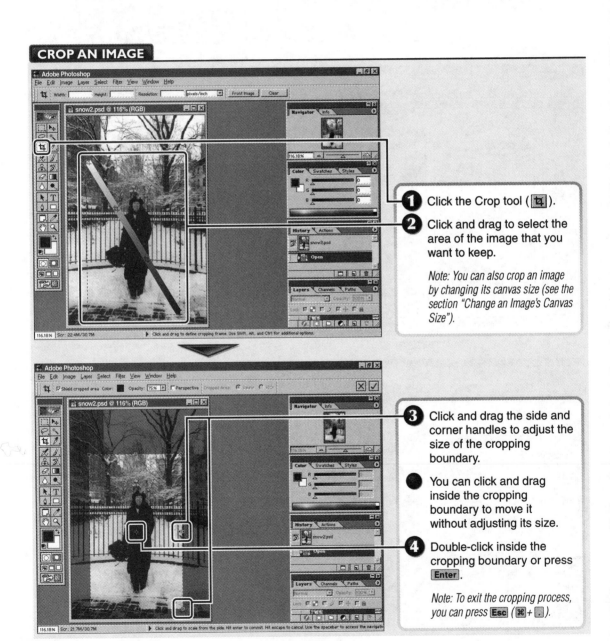

1 Click the Crop tool (■).

2 Click and drag to select the area of the image that you want to keep.

Note: You can also crop an image by changing its canvas size (see the section "Change an Image's Canvas Size").

3 Click and drag the side and corner handles to adjust the size of the cropping boundary.

● You can click and drag inside the cropping boundary to move it without adjusting its size.

4 Double-click inside the cropping boundary or press **Enter**.

*Note: To exit the cropping process, you can press **Esc** (⌘+ .).*

in an instant

Photoshop crops the image, deleting the pixels outside of the cropping boundary.

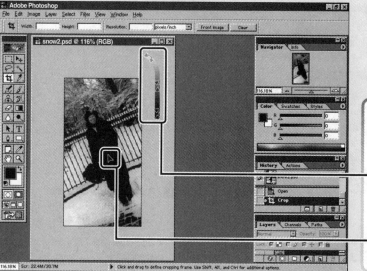

ROTATE THE CROPPING AREA

1 Perform steps **1** through **3** earlier in this section.

2 Click and drag outside of the boundary lines. Photoshop rotates the cropping boundary.

3 Double-click inside the cropping boundary.

DETERMINE AN IMAGE'S SAVED FILE SIZE

You can easily determine the file size of an image
after you have saved it in Photoshop.

DETERMINE FILE SIZE IN WINDOWS

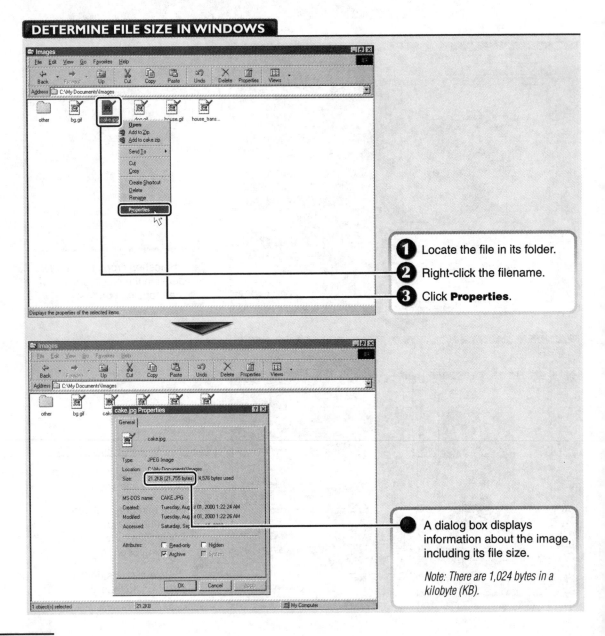

1 Locate the file in its folder.

2 Right-click the filename.

3 Click **Properties**.

A dialog box displays
information about the image,
including its file size.

*Note: There are 1,024 bytes in a
kilobyte (KB).*

in an *instant*

DETERMINE FILE SIZE ON A MACINTOSH

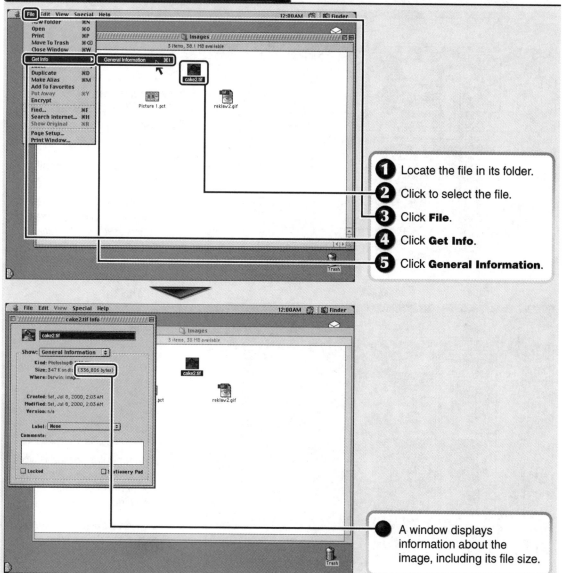

1 Locate the file in its folder.

2 Click to select the file.

3 Click **File**.

4 Click **Get Info**.

5 Click **General Information**.

⬤ A window displays information about the image, including its file size.

SELECT WITH THE MARQUEE TOOLS

You can select a rectangular or elliptical area of your image by using the Marquee tools. Then you can move, delete, or stylize the selected area by using other Photoshop commands.

SELECT WITH THE MARQUEE TOOLS

SELECT WITH THE RECTANGULAR MARQUEE TOOL

1 Click the Rectangular Marquee tool ( ).

2 Click and drag diagonally inside the image window.

Note: You can hold down **Shift** *while you click and drag to create a square selection or hold down* **Alt** *(* **option** *) to create the selection from the center out.*

A rectangular portion of your image is selected. Now you can perform commands on the selected area.

*Note: You can deselect a selection by clicking **Select** and then **Deselect**.*

in an *instant*

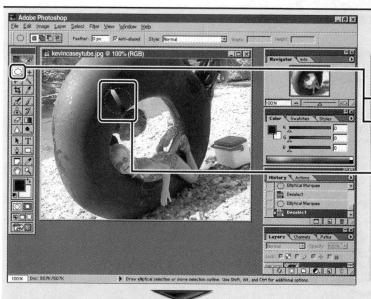

① Click and hold [□].

② In the box that appears, click
the Elliptical Marquee tool
([○]).

③ Click and drag diagonally
inside the image window.

Note: You can hold down **Shift**
*while you click and drag to create
a circular selection or hold down*
Alt *(* **option** *) to create the
selection from the center out.*

● An elliptical portion of your
image is selected. Now you
can perform commands on
the selected area.

SELECT ALL THE PIXELS IN AN IMAGE

You can select all the pixels in an image by using a single command — All. This lets you perform a command on the entire image, such as copying it to a different image window.

SELECT ALL THE PIXELS IN AN IMAGE

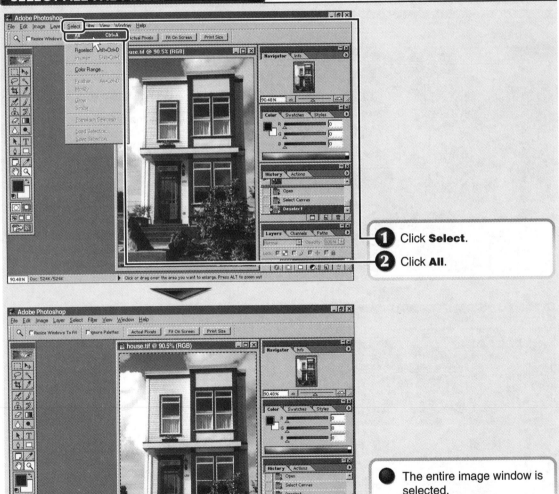

1 Click **Select**.

2 Click **All**.

The entire image window is selected.

Note: With the entire image window selected, you can easily delete your image (by pressing Delete *) or copy and paste it into another window.*

You can move a selection border if your original selection is
not in the intended place.

MOVE A SELECTION BORDER

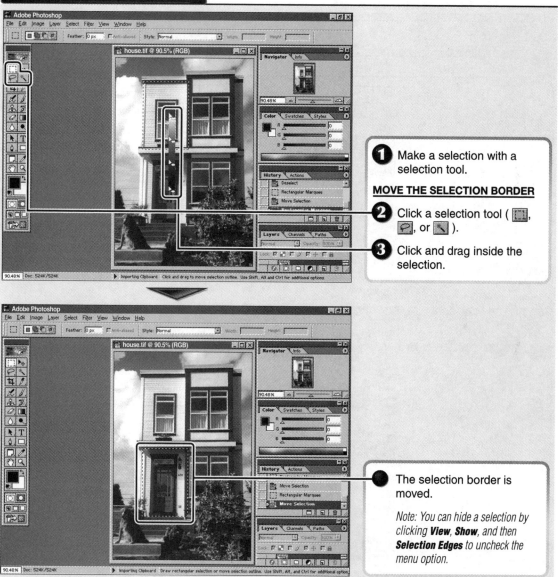

1 Make a selection with a
selection tool.

MOVE THE SELECTION BORDER

2 Click a selection tool (▨,
◯, or ◣).

3 Click and drag inside the
selection.

● The selection border is
moved.

*Note: You can hide a selection by
clicking View, Show, and then
Selection Edges to uncheck the
menu option.*

SELECT WITH THE LASSO TOOL

You can create oddly shaped selections with the Lasso tool. Then you can move, delete, or stylize the selected area by using other Photoshop commands.

SELECT WITH THE LASSO TOOL

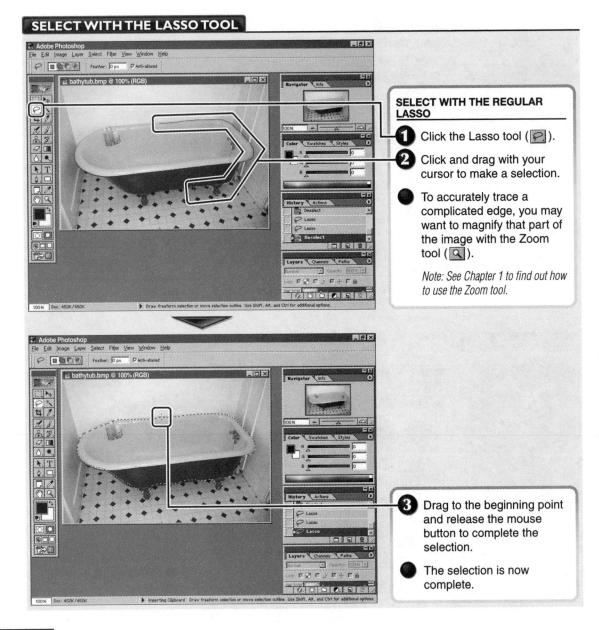

SELECT WITH THE REGULAR LASSO

1. Click the Lasso tool ( ).

2. Click and drag with your cursor to make a selection.

● To accurately trace a complicated edge, you may want to magnify that part of the image with the Zoom tool ( ).

Note: See Chapter 1 to find out how to use the Zoom tool.

3. Drag to the beginning point and release the mouse button to complete the selection.

● The selection is now complete.

in an *instant*

SELECT WITH THE POLYGONAL LASSO

Note: The Polygonal Lasso tool lets you easily create a selection made up of many straight lines.

1 Click and hold 🔲 and select the Polygonal Lasso tool (🔲) from the box that appears.

2 Click multiple times along the border of the area that you want to select.

3 Click the starting point to complete the selection.

Note: If you double-click anywhere in the image, Photoshop will add a final straight line connected to the starting point.

● The selection is now complete.

*Note: You can get a polygonal effect with the regular Lasso tool by pressing **Alt** (**option**) and clicking to make your selection.*

SELECT WITH THE MAGNETIC LASSO TOOL

You can select elements of your image that have well-defined edges quickly and easily with the Magnetic Lasso tool. The Magnetic Lasso tool works best when the element that you are selecting contrasts with its background.

SELECT WITH THE MAGNETIC LASSO TOOL

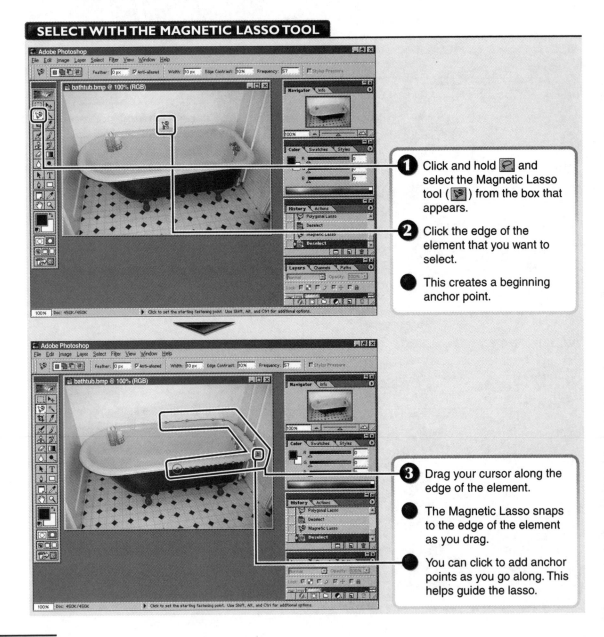

1 Click and hold ⬚ and select the Magnetic Lasso tool (⬚) from the box that appears.

2 Click the edge of the element that you want to select.

● This creates a beginning anchor point.

3 Drag your cursor along the edge of the element.

● The Magnetic Lasso snaps to the edge of the element as you drag.

● You can click to add anchor points as you go along. This helps guide the lasso.

in an instant

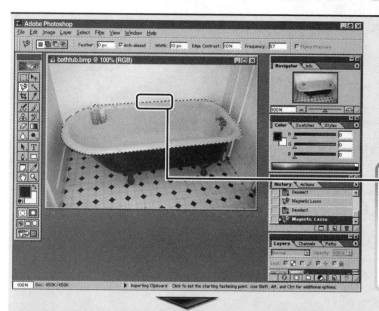

4 Click on the beginning anchor point to finish your selection.

● Alternatively, you can double-click anywhere in the image. Photoshop completes the selection for you.

● The Magnetic Lasso is less useful for selecting areas of an image where there is little contrast.

SELECT WITH THE MAGIC WAND TOOL

You can select groups of similarly colored pixels
with the Magic Wand tool. How similar a pixel
has to be depends on the Tolerance value that
you choose.

SELECT WITH THE MAGIC WAND TOOL

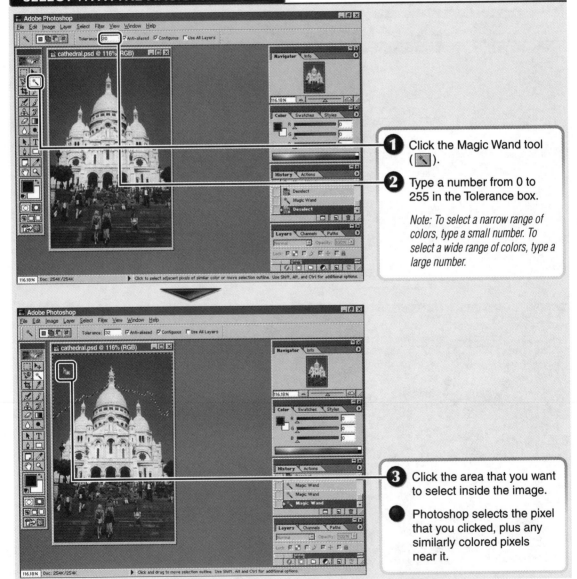

1 Click the Magic Wand tool
( ).

2 Type a number from 0 to
255 in the Tolerance box.

*Note: To select a narrow range of
colors, type a small number. To
select a wide range of colors, type a
large number.*

3 Click the area that you want
to select inside the image.

● Photoshop selects the pixel
that you clicked, plus any
similarly colored pixels
near it.

in an instant

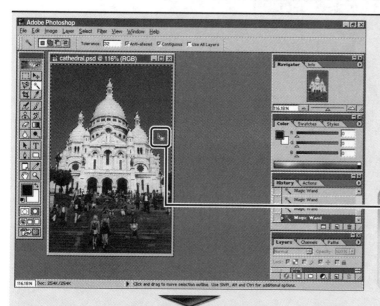

4 To add to your selection,
press **Shift** and click
elsewhere in the image.

● Photoshop adds to your
selection.

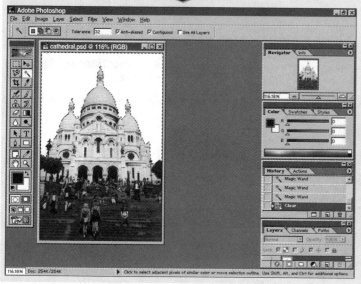

*Note: The Magic Wand tool offers a
quick way to separate an element
from its background.*

● To delete the selected
pixels, you can press **Delete**.

● The pixels are replaced with
the background color (in
this case, white).

SELECT WITH THE COLOR RANGE COMMAND

You can select a set range of colors with the Color Range command. This allows you to quickly select a region of relatively solid color in an image, such as a sky or a blank wall.

SELECT WITH THE COLOR RANGE COMMAND

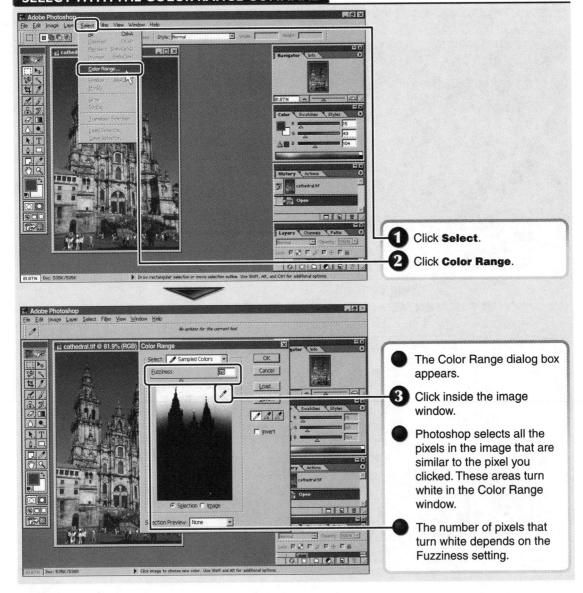

1 Click **Select**.

2 Click **Color Range**.

● The Color Range dialog box appears.

3 Click inside the image window.

● Photoshop selects all the pixels in the image that are similar to the pixel you clicked. These areas turn white in the Color Range window.

● The number of pixels that turn white depends on the Fuzziness setting.

in an *instant*

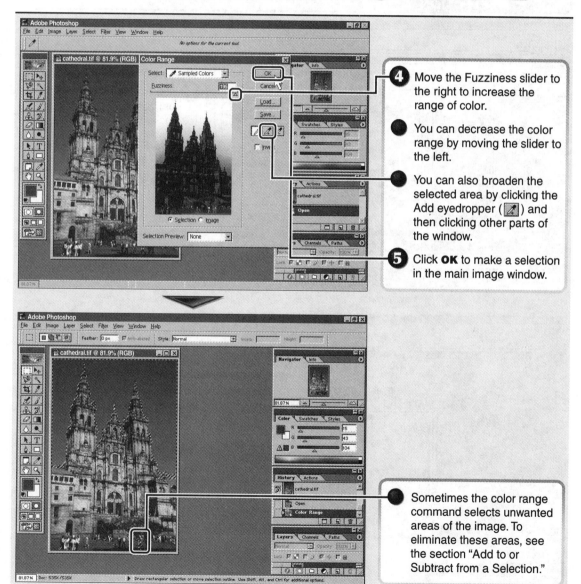

4 Move the Fuzziness slider to the right to increase the range of color.

● You can decrease the color range by moving the slider to the left.

● You can also broaden the selected area by clicking the Add eyedropper ( ) and then clicking other parts of the window.

5 Click **OK** to make a selection in the main image window.

● Sometimes the color range command selects unwanted areas of the image. To eliminate these areas, see the section "Add to or Subtract from a Selection."

You can add to or subtract from your
selection by using various selection tools.

ADD TO A SELECTION

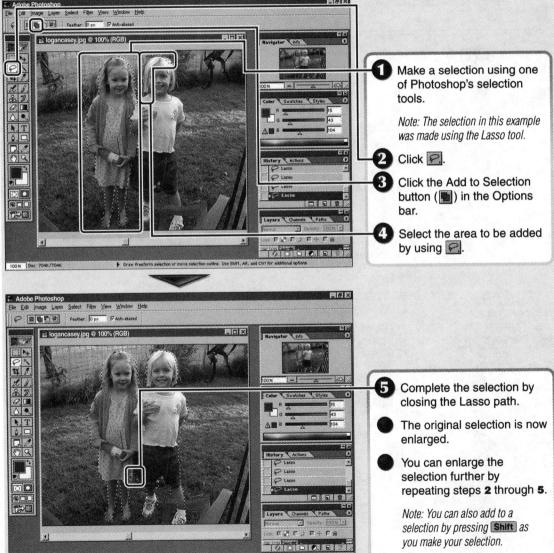

1 Make a selection using one
of Photoshop's selection
tools.

*Note: The selection in this example
was made using the Lasso tool.*

2 Click [icon].

3 Click the Add to Selection
button ([icon]) in the Options
bar.

4 Select the area to be added
by using [icon].

5 Complete the selection by
closing the Lasso path.

● The original selection is now
enlarged.

● You can enlarge the
selection further by
repeating steps **2** through **5**.

*Note: You can also add to a
selection by pressing* **Shift** *as
you make your selection.*

in an instant

SUBTRACT FROM A SELECTION

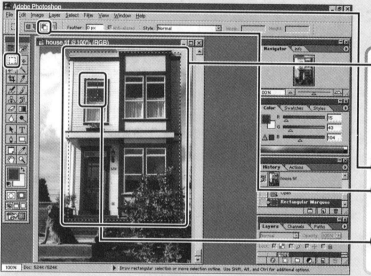

① Make a selection using one of Photoshop's selection tools.

Note: The selection in this example was made with the Rectangular Marquee tool.

② Click 🔲.

③ Click the Subtract from Selection button (🔲) in the Options bar.

④ Select the area to be subtracted.

● Any part of the original selection that is part of the new selection is deselected (subtracted).

● You can subtract other parts of the selection by repeating steps **2** through **4**.

Note: You can also subtract from a selection by holding down **Alt** *(* **option** *) as you make your selection.*

49

EXPAND OR CONTRACT SELECTIONS

You can expand or contract a selection by a set number of pixels. This lets you easily fine-tune your selections.

EXPAND A SELECTION

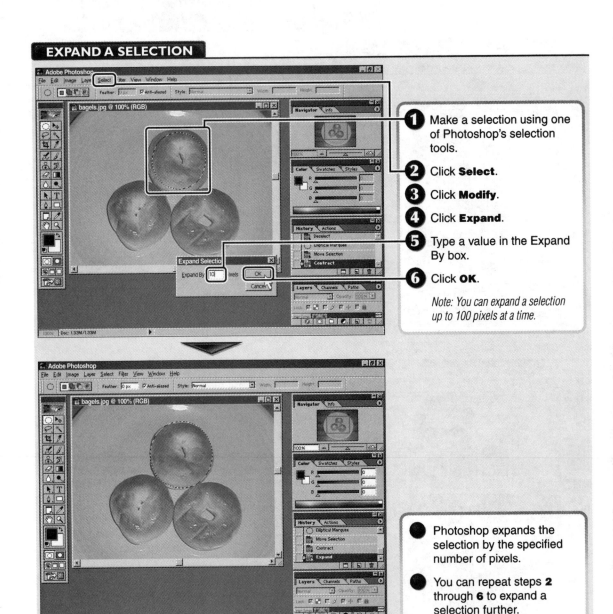

1 Make a selection using one of Photoshop's selection tools.

2 Click **Select**.

3 Click **Modify**.

4 Click **Expand**.

5 Type a value in the Expand By box.

6 Click **OK**.

Note: You can expand a selection up to 100 pixels at a time.

■ Photoshop expands the selection by the specified number of pixels.

■ You can repeat steps **2** through **6** to expand a selection further.

in an instant

CONTRACT A SELECTION

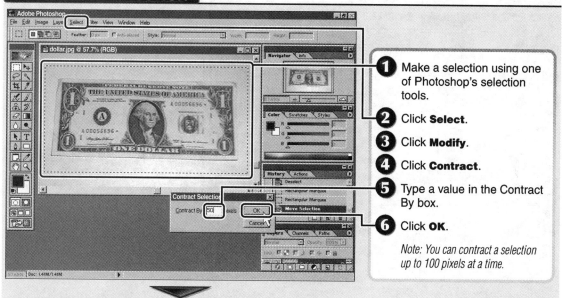

1. Make a selection using one of Photoshop's selection tools.

2. Click **Select**.

3. Click **Modify**.

4. Click **Contract**.

5. Type a value in the Contract By box.

6. Click **OK**.

Note: You can contract a selection up to 100 pixels at a time.

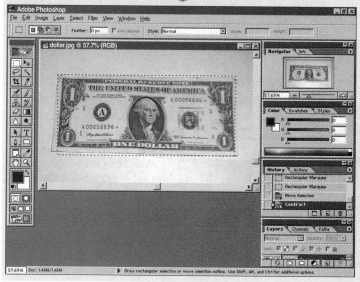

● Photoshop contracts the selection by the number of pixels specified.

● You can repeat steps **2** through **6** to contract a selection further.

USING THE GROW AND SIMILAR COMMANDS

You can increase the size of your selection to include areas with a similar color by using the Grow or Similar command. The Grow command adds pixels contiguous to the current selection, whereas the Similar command adds pixels that are of a similar color anywhere in the image.

USING THE GROW COMMAND

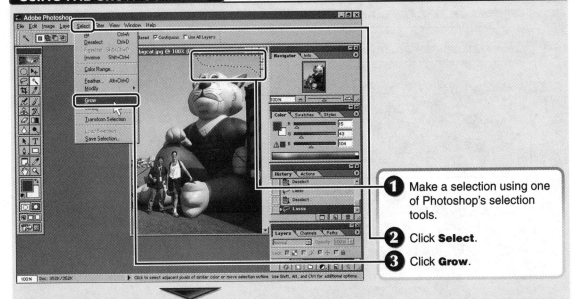

1 Make a selection using one of Photoshop's selection tools.

2 Click **Select**.

3 Click **Grow**.

● The selection expands to include other similarly colored pixels contiguous to the original selection.

Note: Image expansion depends on the Tolerance value for the Magic Wand tool. See "Select with the Magic Wand Tool" earlier in this chapter for details.

in an *instant*

USING THE SIMILAR COMMAND

① Make a selection using one
of Photoshop's selection
tools.

② Click **Select**.

③ Click **Similar**.

● The selection expands to
include other similarly
colored pixels throughout
the image.

*Note: Image expansion depends on
the Tolerance value for the Magic
Wand tool. See "Select with the
Magic Wand Tool" earlier in this
chapter for details.*

MOVE A SELECTION

You can move a selection in the background or another layer by using the Move tool. This lets you rearrange elements of your image.

MOVE A SELECTION

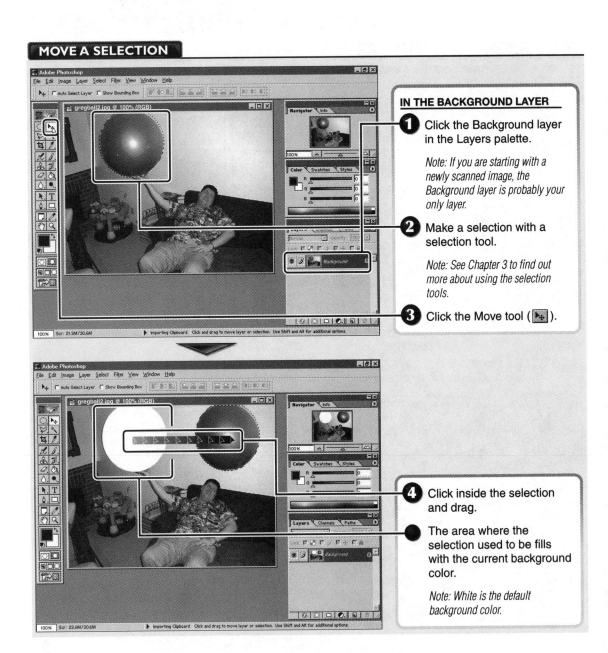

IN THE BACKGROUND LAYER

1 Click the Background layer in the Layers palette.

Note: If you are starting with a newly scanned image, the Background layer is probably your only layer.

2 Make a selection with a selection tool.

Note: See Chapter 3 to find out more about using the selection tools.

3 Click the Move tool ( ).

4 Click inside the selection and drag.

The area where the selection used to be fills with the current background color.

Note: White is the default background color.

in an

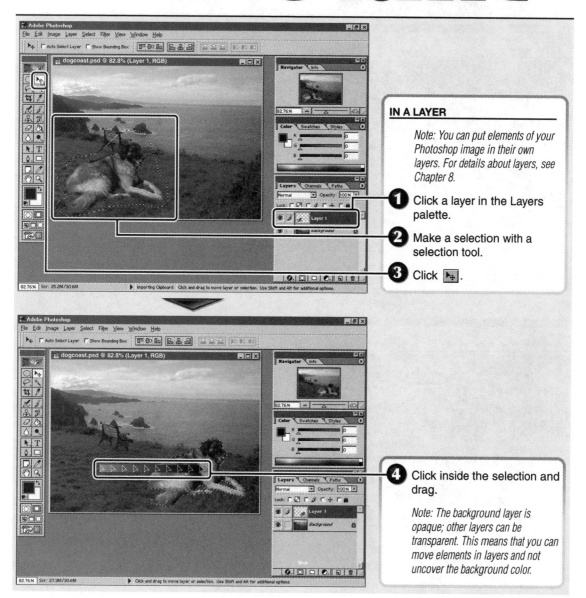

IN A LAYER

Note: You can put elements of your Photoshop image in their own layers. For details about layers, see Chapter 8.

① Click a layer in the Layers palette.

② Make a selection with a selection tool.

③ Click 🔄.

④ Click inside the selection and drag.

Note: The background layer is opaque; other layers can be transparent. This means that you can move elements in layers and not uncover the background color.

COPY AND PASTE A SELECTION

You can copy a selection and paste a duplicate
of it somewhere else in the image.

COPY AND PASTE A SELECTION

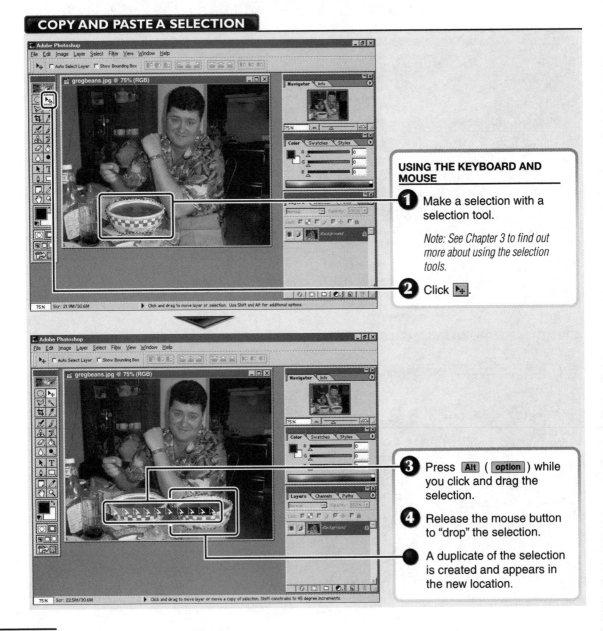

**USING THE KEYBOARD AND
MOUSE**

1 Make a selection with a
selection tool.

*Note: See Chapter 3 to find out
more about using the selection
tools.*

2 Click ▶₊.

3 Press **Alt** (**option**) while
you click and drag the
selection.

4 Release the mouse button
to "drop" the selection.

● A duplicate of the selection
is created and appears in
the new location.

in an *instant*

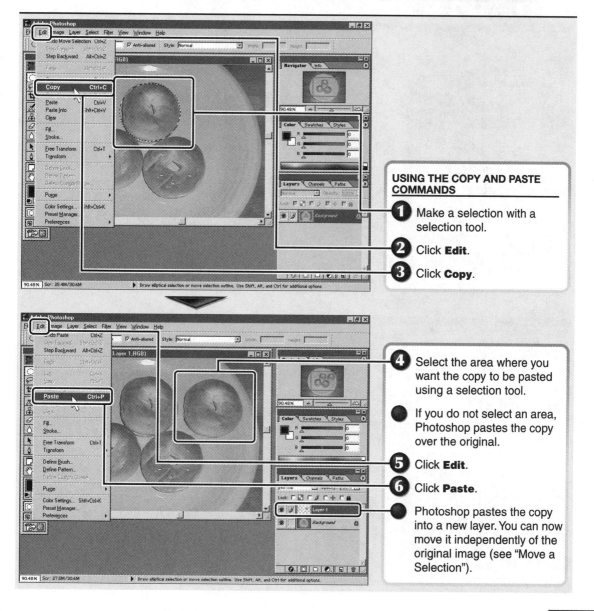

USING THE COPY AND PASTE COMMANDS

1 Make a selection with a selection tool.

2 Click **Edit**.

3 Click **Copy**.

4 Select the area where you want the copy to be pasted using a selection tool.

● If you do not select an area, Photoshop pastes the copy over the original.

5 Click **Edit**.

6 Click **Paste**.

● Photoshop pastes the copy into a new layer. You can now move it independently of the original image (see "Move a Selection").

DELETE A SELECTION

You can delete a selection to remove elements from your image.

DELETE A SELECTION

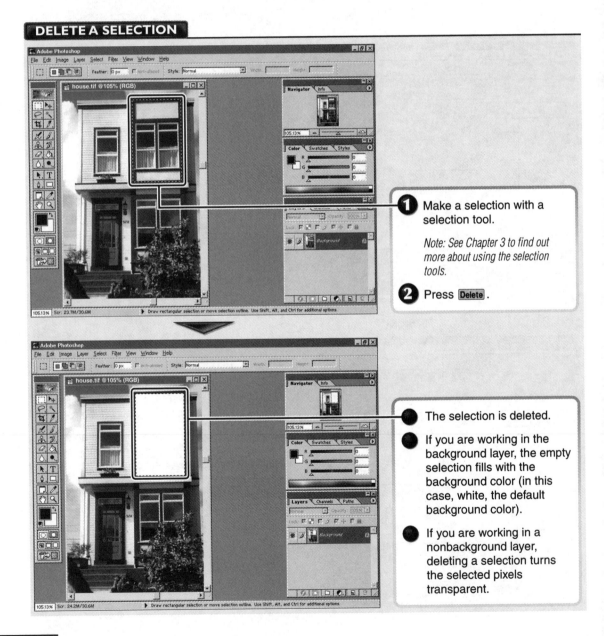

1 Make a selection with a selection tool.

Note: See Chapter 3 to find out more about using the selection tools.

2 Press Delete .

● The selection is deleted.

● If you are working in the background layer, the empty selection fills with the background color (in this case, white, the default background color).

● If you are working in a nonbackground layer, deleting a selection turns the selected pixels transparent.

FLIP A SELECTION

You can flip a selection horizontally or
vertically to reverse the orientation of
an element in your image.

FLIP A SELECTION

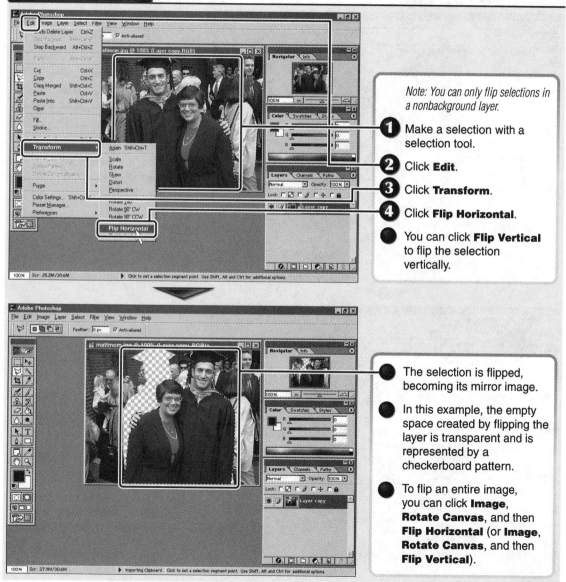

*Note: You can only flip selections in
a nonbackground layer.*

1 Make a selection with a
selection tool.

2 Click **Edit**.

3 Click **Transform**.

4 Click **Flip Horizontal**.

● You can click **Flip Vertical**
to flip the selection
vertically.

● The selection is flipped,
becoming its mirror image.

● In this example, the empty
space created by flipping the
layer is transparent and is
represented by a
checkerboard pattern.

● To flip an entire image,
you can click **Image**,
Rotate Canvas, and then
Flip Horizontal (or **Image**,
Rotate Canvas, and then
Flip Vertical).

ROTATE A SELECTION

You can rotate a selection to tilt an element in your image or to turn it upside down.

ROTATE A SELECTION

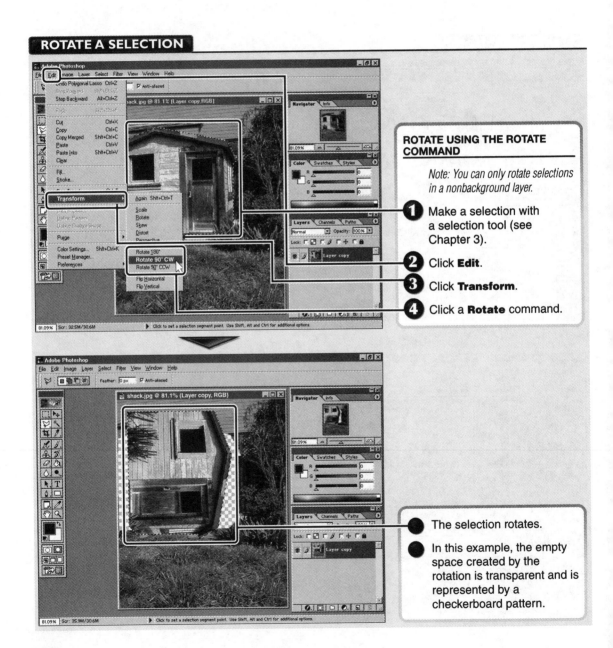

ROTATE USING THE ROTATE COMMAND

Note: You can only rotate selections in a nonbackground layer.

1 Make a selection with a selection tool (see Chapter 3).

2 Click **Edit**.

3 Click **Transform**.

4 Click a **Rotate** command.

● The selection rotates.

● In this example, the empty space created by the rotation is transparent and is represented by a checkerboard pattern.

in an *instant*

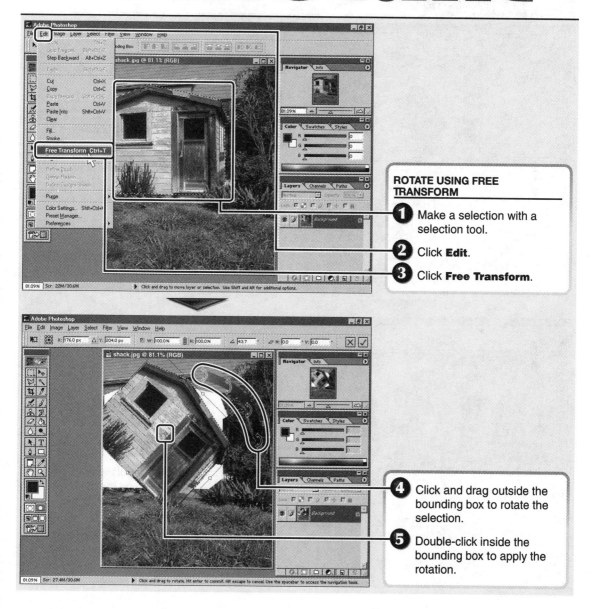

ROTATE USING FREE TRANSFORM

1 Make a selection with a selection tool.

2 Click **Edit**.

3 Click **Free Transform**.

4 Click and drag outside the bounding box to rotate the selection.

5 Double-click inside the bounding box to apply the rotation.

SCALE A SELECTION

You can scale a selection to make it larger
or smaller.

SCALE A SELECTION

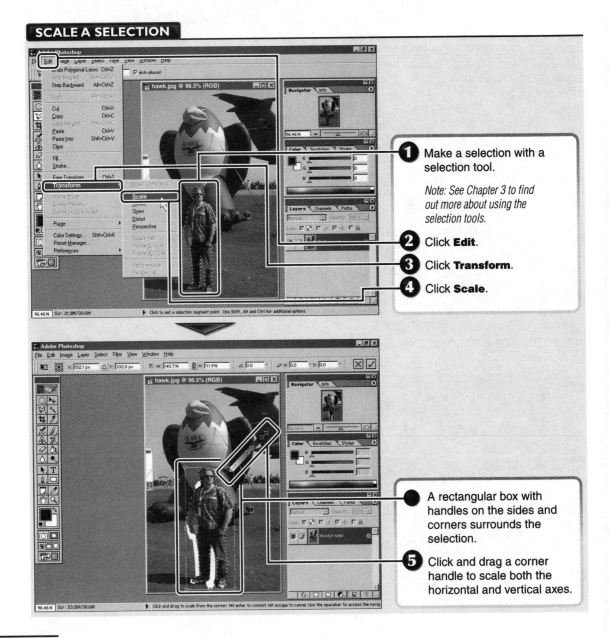

1 Make a selection with a
selection tool.

*Note: See Chapter 3 to find
out more about using the
selection tools.*

2 Click **Edit**.

3 Click **Transform**.

4 Click **Scale**.

A rectangular box with
handles on the sides and
corners surrounds the
selection.

5 Click and drag a corner
handle to scale both the
horizontal and vertical axes.

in an instant

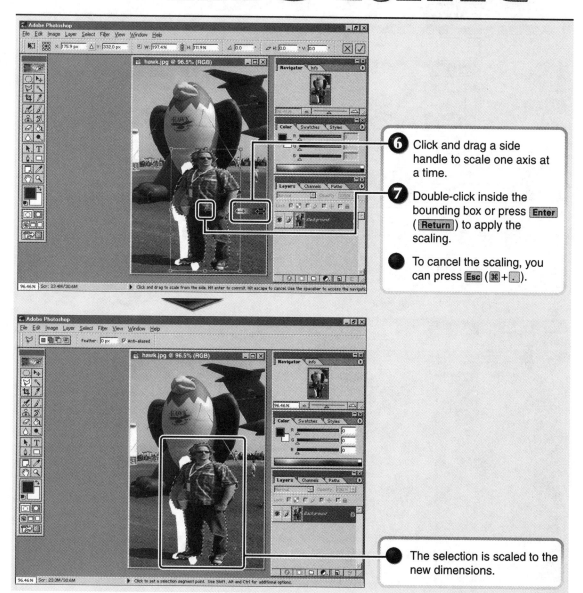

6 Click and drag a side handle to scale one axis at a time.

7 Double-click inside the bounding box or press `Enter` (`Return`) to apply the scaling.

● To cancel the scaling, you can press `Esc` (`⌘`+`.`).

● The selection is scaled to the new dimensions.

SKEW OR DISTORT A SELECTION

You can transform a selection by using the Skew or Distort command. This lets you stretch elements in your image into interesting shapes.

SKEW A SELECTION

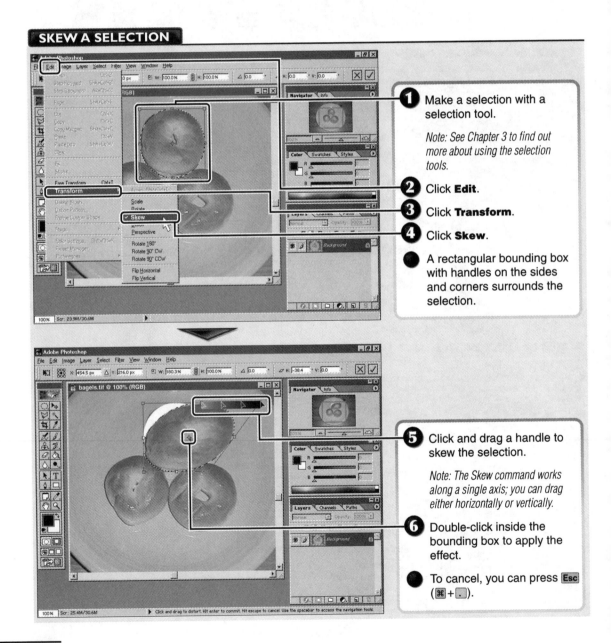

1 Make a selection with a selection tool.

Note: See Chapter 3 to find out more about using the selection tools.

2 Click **Edit**.

3 Click **Transform**.

4 Click **Skew**.

● A rectangular bounding box with handles on the sides and corners surrounds the selection.

5 Click and drag a handle to skew the selection.

Note: The Skew command works along a single axis; you can drag either horizontally or vertically.

6 Double-click inside the bounding box to apply the effect.

● To cancel, you can press Esc (⌘+.).

in an *instant*

DISTORT A SELECTION

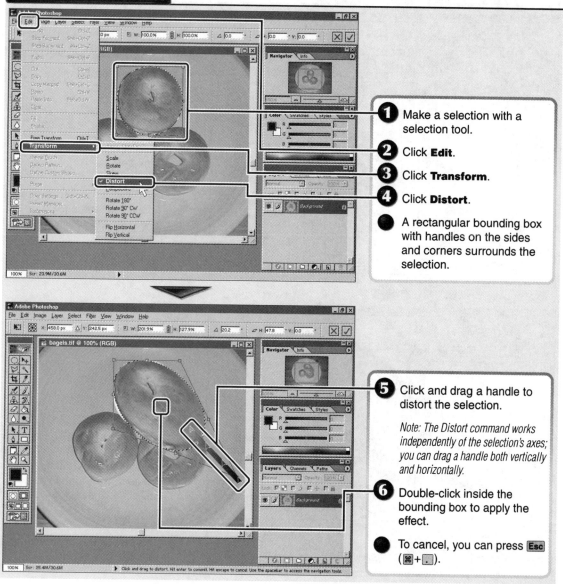

1 Make a selection with a selection tool.

2 Click **Edit**.

3 Click **Transform**.

4 Click **Distort**.

● A rectangular bounding box with handles on the sides and corners surrounds the selection.

5 Click and drag a handle to distort the selection.

Note: The Distort command works independently of the selection's axes; you can drag a handle both vertically and horizontally.

6 Double-click inside the bounding box to apply the effect.

● To cancel, you can press Esc (⌘+.).

FEATHER THE SELECTION BORDER

You can feather a selection's border to create soft edges.

FEATHER THE SELECTION BORDER

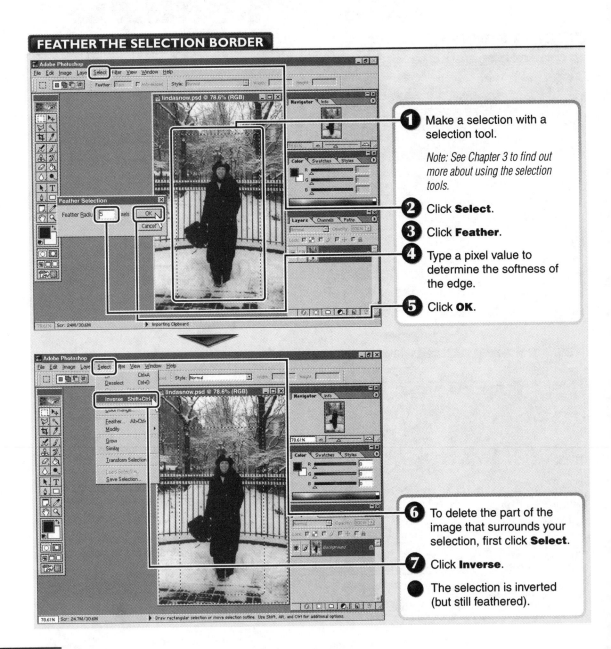

① Make a selection with a selection tool.

Note: See Chapter 3 to find out more about using the selection tools.

② Click **Select**.

③ Click **Feather**.

④ Type a pixel value to determine the softness of the edge.

⑤ Click **OK**.

⑥ To delete the part of the image that surrounds your selection, first click **Select**.

⑦ Click **Inverse**.

● The selection is inverted (but still feathered).

in an instant

8 Press `Delete`.

● By deleting the surrounding pixels, you can see the effect of the feathering.

● The image in this example was feathered with a large pixel value (20 pixels).

Note: To automate this feathering effect, see "Create a Vignette Effect" in Chapter 12.

USING THE RUBBER STAMP TOOL

You can clean up small flaws or overwrite elements in your image with the Rubber Stamp tool. The tool copies information from one area of an image to another.

USING THE RUBBER STAMP TOOL

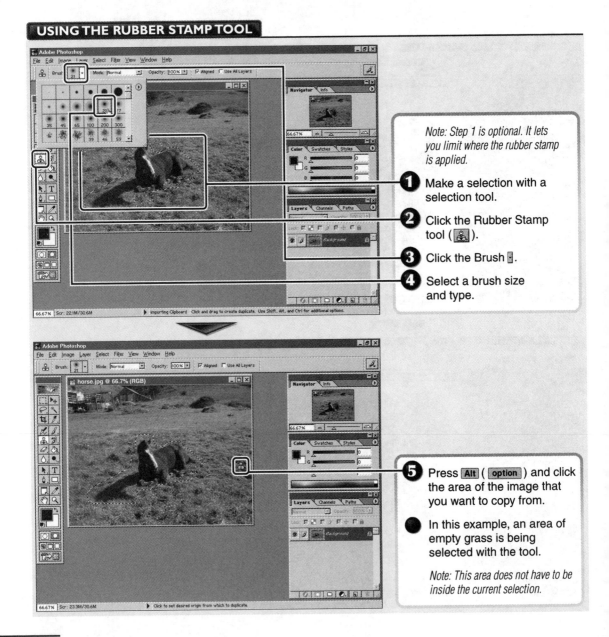

Note: Step 1 is optional. It lets you limit where the rubber stamp is applied.

1 Make a selection with a selection tool.

2 Click the Rubber Stamp tool ( ).

3 Click the Brush .

4 Select a brush size and type.

5 Press Alt (option) and click the area of the image that you want to copy from.

● In this example, an area of empty grass is being selected with the tool.

Note: This area does not have to be inside the current selection.

in an *instant*

6 Click and drag inside the selection to apply the rubber stamp.

● The area is copied to where you click and drag.

7 Click and drag repeatedly over the area to achieve the desired effect.

● In this example, the image of the horse has been copied over by the grass selection.

USING THE ERASER TOOL

You can make parts of your image disappear with the Eraser tool, which turns pixels in your layers transparent. The Eraser tool has no effect on an image's background layer.

USING THE ERASER TOOL

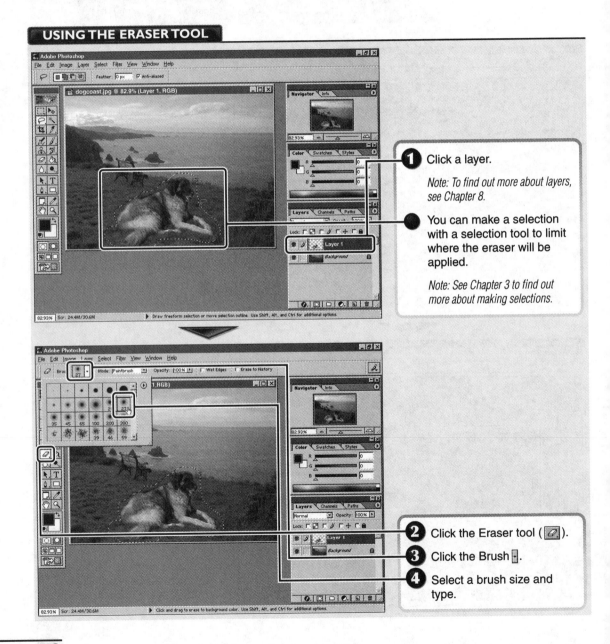

1 Click a layer.

Note: To find out more about layers, see Chapter 8.

You can make a selection with a selection tool to limit where the eraser will be applied.

Note: See Chapter 3 to find out more about making selections.

2 Click the Eraser tool ( ).

3 Click the Brush .

4 Select a brush size and type.

in an *instant*

5 Click and drag inside the selection.

● The tool turns areas of the layer transparent.

● The tool has no effect on the background layer.

USING THE MAGIC ERASER TOOL

You can quickly turn large areas of a layer transparent with the Magic
Eraser tool.

USING THE MAGIC ERASER TOOL

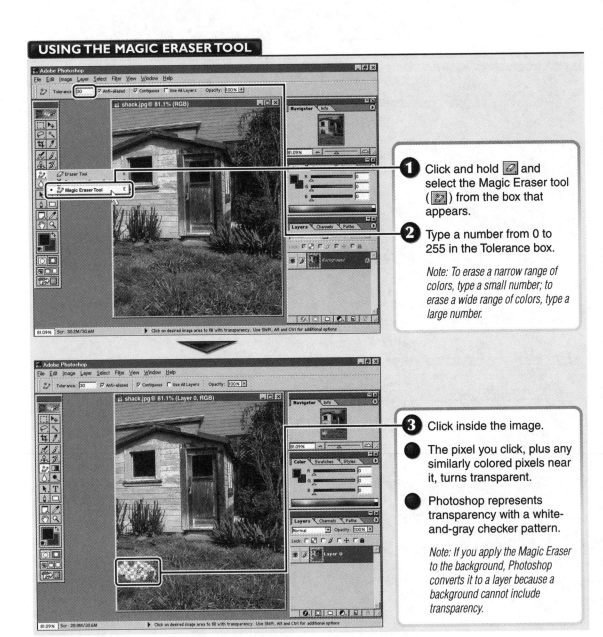

1 Click and hold ☑ and
select the Magic Eraser tool
(☑) from the box that
appears.

2 Type a number from 0 to
255 in the Tolerance box.

*Note: To erase a narrow range of
colors, type a small number; to
erase a wide range of colors, type a
large number.*

3 Click inside the image.

● The pixel you click, plus any
similarly colored pixels near
it, turns transparent.

● Photoshop represents
transparency with a white-
and-gray checker pattern.

*Note: If you apply the Magic Eraser
to the background, Photoshop
converts it to a layer because a
background cannot include
transparency.*

in an *instant*

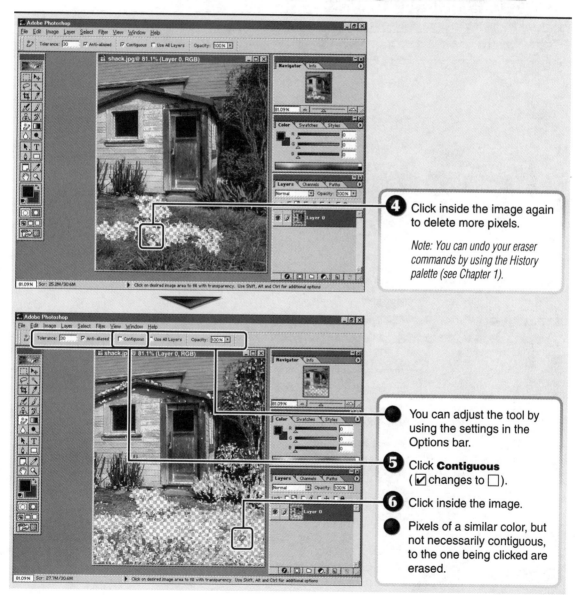

4 Click inside the image again to delete more pixels.

Note: You can undo your eraser commands by using the History palette (see Chapter 1).

You can adjust the tool by using the settings in the Options bar.

5 Click **Contiguous** (☑ changes to ☐).

6 Click inside the image.

Pixels of a similar color, but not necessarily contiguous, to the one being clicked are erased.

USING THE EXTRACT COMMAND

You can remove an element in an image from its background by using the Extract command.

USING THE EXTRACT COMMAND

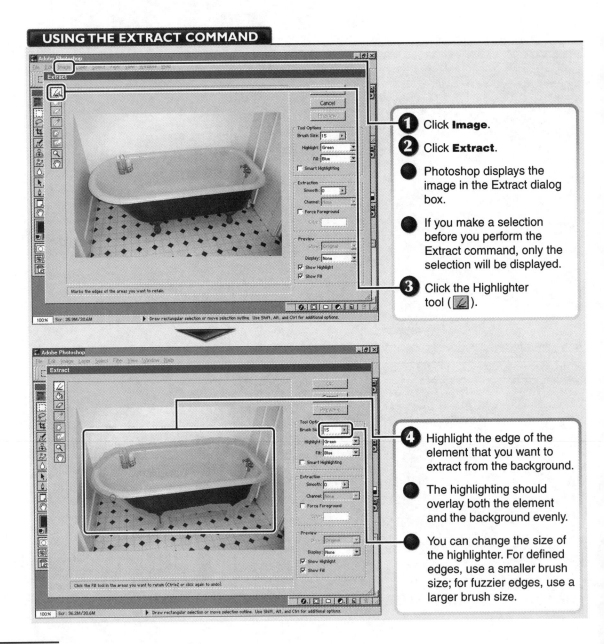

1 Click **Image**.

2 Click **Extract**.

● Photoshop displays the image in the Extract dialog box.

● If you make a selection before you perform the Extract command, only the selection will be displayed.

3 Click the Highlighter tool ( ).

4 Highlight the edge of the element that you want to extract from the background.

● The highlighting should overlay both the element and the background evenly.

● You can change the size of the highlighter. For defined edges, use a smaller brush size; for fuzzier edges, use a larger brush size.

in an *instant*

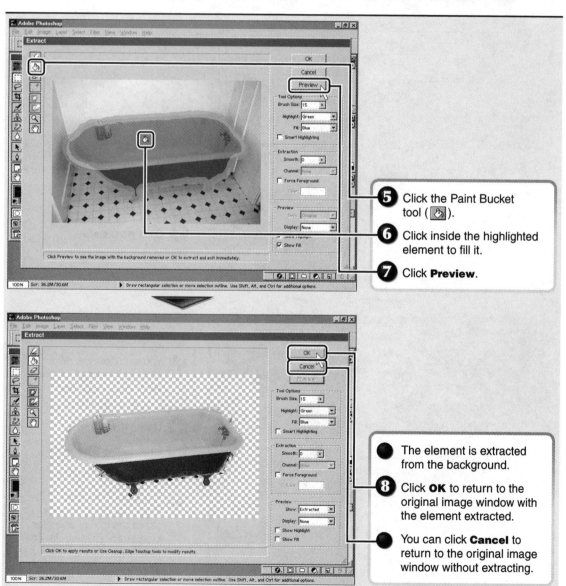

5 Click the Paint Bucket
tool ( ).

6 Click inside the highlighted
element to fill it.

7 Click **Preview**.

● The element is extracted
from the background.

8 Click **OK** to return to the
original image window with
the element extracted.

● You can click **Cancel** to
return to the original image
window without extracting.

You can work with a color image in RGB mode. RGB is the most common mode for working with color images in Photoshop. RGB stands for Red, Green, Blue. In RGB mode, the image is stored as a combination of these three primary colors.

WORK IN RGB MODE

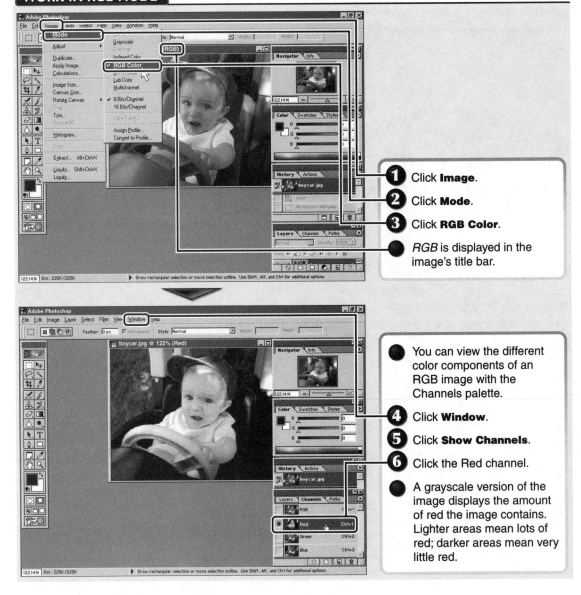

1 Click **Image**.

2 Click **Mode**.

3 Click **RGB Color**.

● *RGB* is displayed in the image's title bar.

● You can view the different color components of an RGB image with the Channels palette.

4 Click **Window**.

5 Click **Show Channels**.

6 Click the Red channel.

● A grayscale version of the image displays the amount of red the image contains. Lighter areas mean lots of red; darker areas mean very little red.

in an *instant*

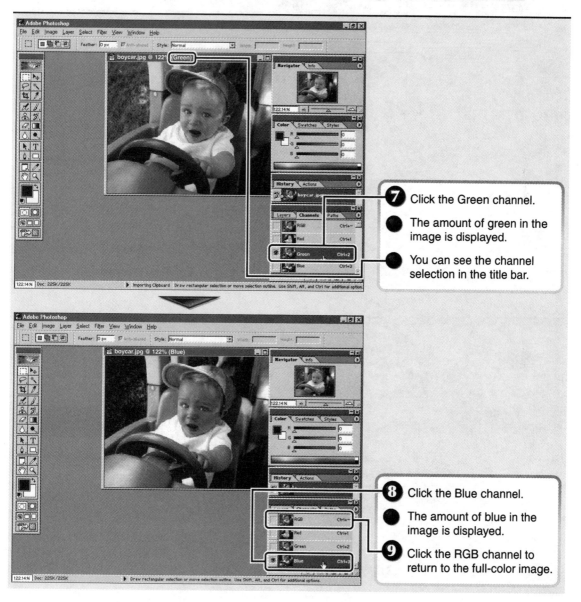

7 Click the Green channel.

● The amount of green in the image is displayed.

● You can see the channel selection in the title bar.

8 Click the Blue channel.

● The amount of blue in the image is displayed.

9 Click the RGB channel to return to the full-color image.

CONVERT COLOR IMAGES TO GRAYSCALE

You can remove the color from your image by converting it to grayscale mode. *Grayscale* images are made up of pixels that are white, gray, and black.

CONVERT COLOR IMAGES TO GRAYSCALE

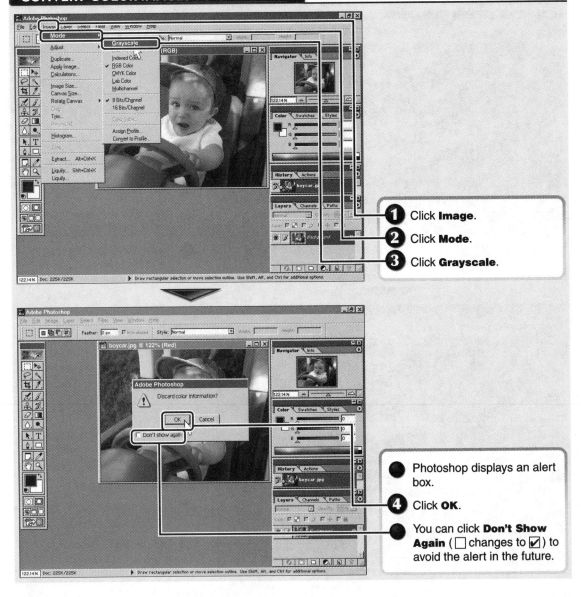

1 Click **Image**.

2 Click **Mode**.

3 Click **Grayscale**.

● Photoshop displays an alert box.

4 Click **OK**.

● You can click **Don't Show Again** (☐ changes to ☑) to avoid the alert in the future.

in an *instant*

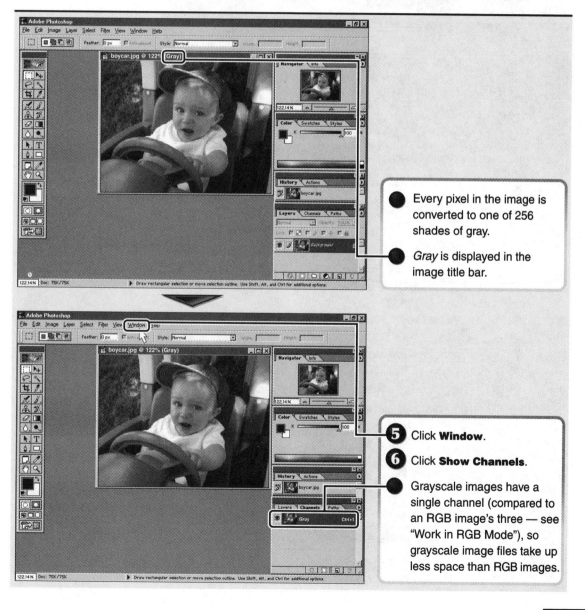

● Every pixel in the image is converted to one of 256 shades of gray.

● *Gray* is displayed in the image title bar.

5 Click **Window**.

6 Click **Show Channels**.

● Grayscale images have a single channel (compared to an RGB image's three — see "Work in RGB Mode"), so grayscale image files take up less space than RGB images.

CREATE A DUOTONE

You can convert a grayscale image to a
duotone. A *duotone* is essentially a
grayscale image with a color tint.

CREATE A DUOTONE

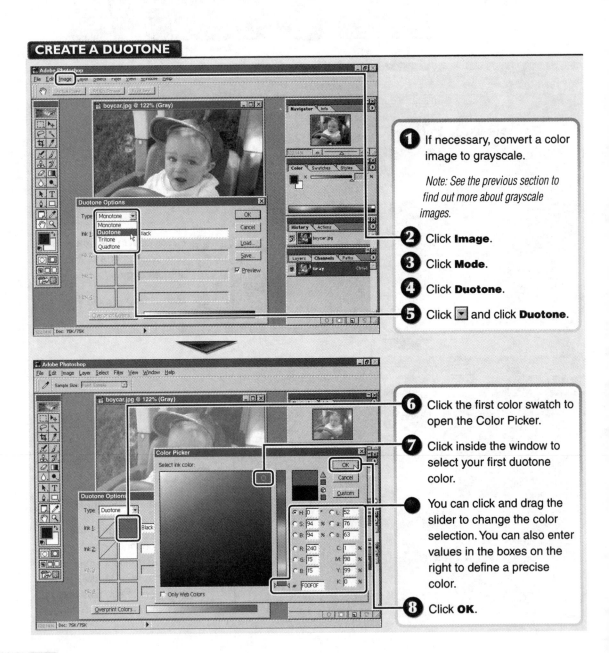

1 If necessary, convert a color
image to grayscale.

*Note: See the previous section to
find out more about grayscale
images.*

2 Click **Image**.

3 Click **Mode**.

4 Click **Duotone**.

5 Click 🔽 and click **Duotone**.

6 Click the first color swatch to
open the Color Picker.

7 Click inside the window to
select your first duotone
color.

● You can click and drag the
slider to change the color
selection. You can also enter
values in the boxes on the
right to define a precise
color.

8 Click **OK**.

in an *instant*

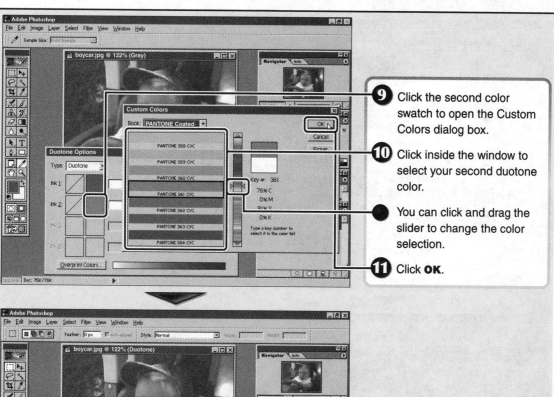

9 Click the second color swatch to open the Custom Colors dialog box.

10 Click inside the window to select your second duotone color.

● You can click and drag the slider to change the color selection.

11 Click **OK**.

12 Click **OK** in the Duotone Options dialog box.

● Photoshop uses the two selected colors to create the tones in the image.

CREATE A BITMAP IMAGE

You can convert a grayscale image to a bitmap image. In Photoshop, a bitmap image is made up of only black-and-white pixels.

CREATE A BITMAP IMAGE

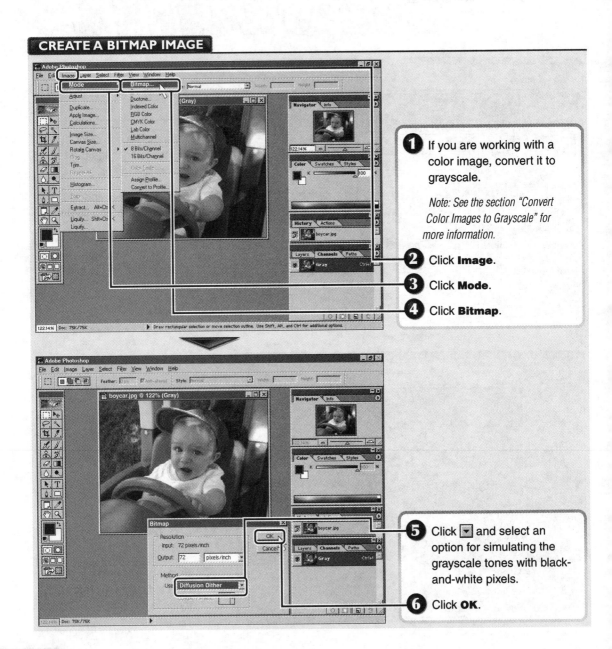

1 If you are working with a color image, convert it to grayscale.

Note: See the section "Convert Color Images to Grayscale" for more information.

2 Click **Image**.

3 Click **Mode**.

4 Click **Bitmap**.

5 Click ⬇ and select an option for simulating the grayscale tones with black-and-white pixels.

6 Click **OK**.

in an *instant*

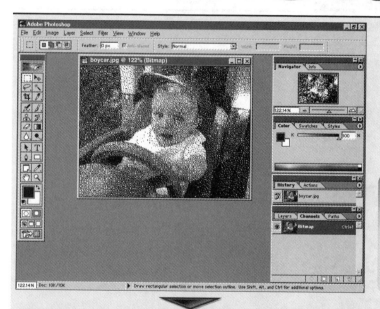

This figure shows the Diffusion Dither option, in which a random mixture of black-and-white pixels simulates the grayscale tones.

This figure shows the 50% Threshold option, in which pixels that are less than 50% black turn to white and pixels that are more than 50% black turn to black.

CREATE AN INDEXED COLOR IMAGE

You can reduce the number of colors that make up an image with the indexed color mode. Use the indexed color mode to prepare GIF images, which contain 256 colors or fewer.

CREATE AN INDEXED COLOR IMAGE

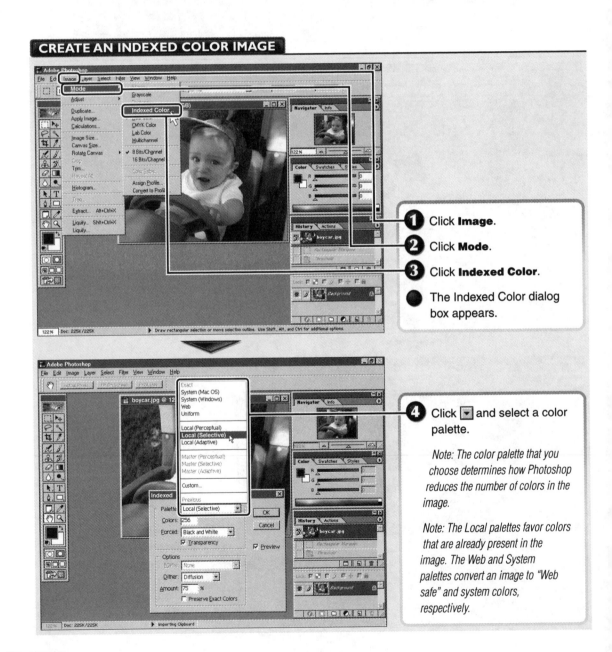

1 Click **Image**.

2 Click **Mode**.

3 Click **Indexed Color**.

● The Indexed Color dialog box appears.

4 Click ▼ and select a color palette.

Note: The color palette that you choose determines how Photoshop reduces the number of colors in the image.

Note: The Local palettes favor colors that are already present in the image. The Web and System palettes convert an image to "Web safe" and system colors, respectively.

in an *instant*

5 Select the number of colors your final image will contain.

Note: More colors produce better-looking images, but fewer colors result in a smaller file size.

6 Click ▼ and select a Dither option.

Note: With dithering on, two colors are mixed to simulate a third. This helps conserve colors and improve quality.

7 Click **OK**.

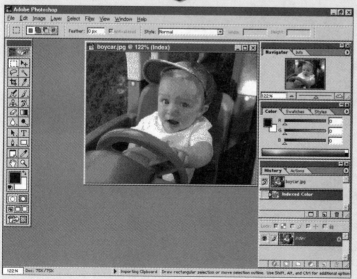

● Photoshop reduces the number of colors in the image to the specified value.

CHOOSE THE FOREGROUND AND BACKGROUND COLORS

You can work with two colors at a time in Photoshop: a foreground color and a background color. Painting tools such as the Paintbrush apply foreground color. Background colors are applied when you use the Eraser tool, enlarge the image canvas, or cut pieces out of your image.

CHOOSE THE FOREGROUND AND BACKGROUND COLORS

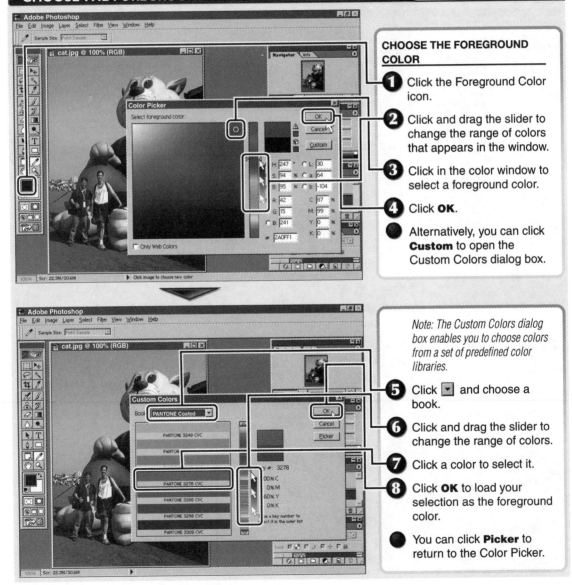

CHOOSE THE FOREGROUND COLOR

1 Click the Foreground Color icon.

2 Click and drag the slider to change the range of colors that appears in the window.

3 Click in the color window to select a foreground color.

4 Click **OK**.

● Alternatively, you can click **Custom** to open the Custom Colors dialog box.

Note: The Custom Colors dialog box enables you to choose colors from a set of predefined color libraries.

5 Click ▼ and choose a book.

6 Click and drag the slider to change the range of colors.

7 Click a color to select it.

8 Click **OK** to load your selection as the foreground color.

● You can click **Picker** to return to the Color Picker.

in an *instant*

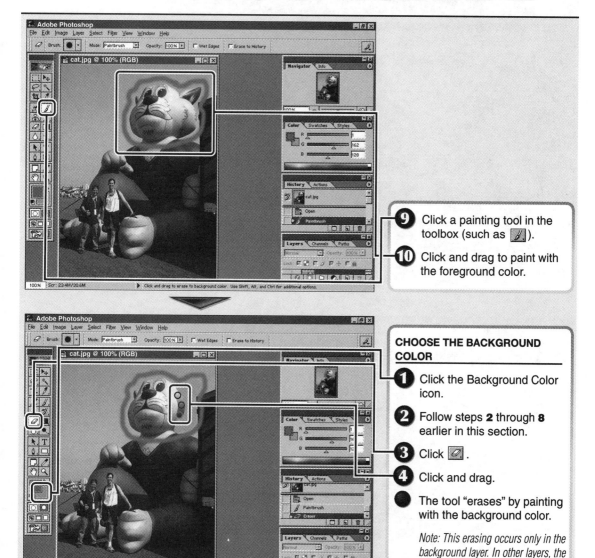

9 Click a painting tool in the toolbox (such as).

10 Click and drag to paint with the foreground color.

CHOOSE THE BACKGROUND COLOR

1 Click the Background Color icon.

2 Follow steps **2** through **8** earlier in this section.

3 Click .

4 Click and drag.

● The tool "erases" by painting with the background color.

Note: This erasing occurs only in the background layer. In other layers, the eraser turns pixels transparent.

SELECT A COLOR WITH THE EYEDROPPER TOOL

You can select a color from an open image with the Eyedropper tool. The Eyedropper tool enables you to paint using a color already present in your image.

SELECT A COLOR WITH THE EYEDROPPER TOOL

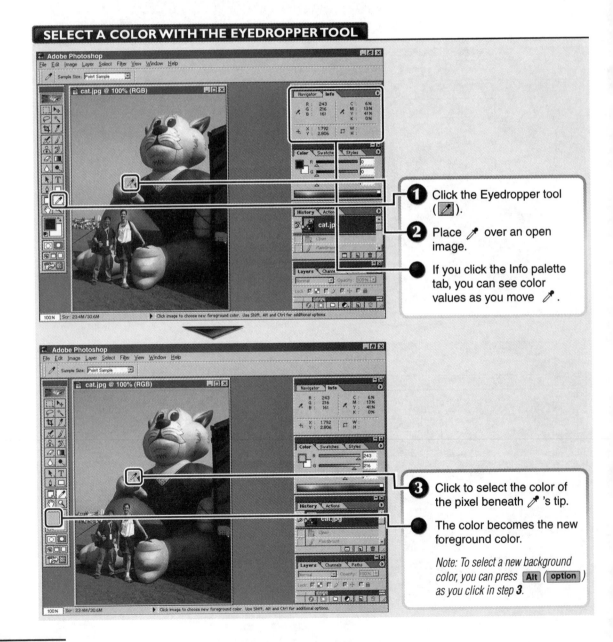

1 Click the Eyedropper tool ( ).

2 Place over an open image.

■ If you click the Info palette tab, you can see color values as you move .

3 Click to select the color of the pixel beneath 's tip.

■ The color becomes the new foreground color.

Note: To select a new background color, you can press Alt (option) as you click in step 3.

SELECT A COLOR WITH THE COLOR PALETTE

You can select a color for your images by using the Color palette.

SELECT A COLOR WITH THE COLOR PALETTE

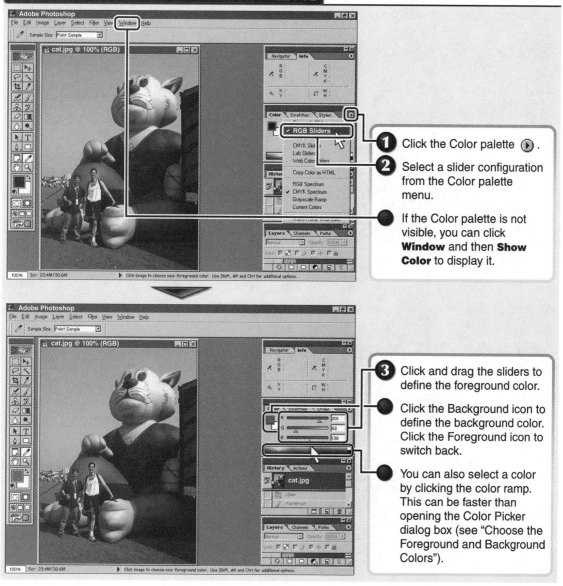

① Click the Color palette ⊙.

② Select a slider configuration from the Color palette menu.

● If the Color palette is not visible, you can click **Window** and then **Show Color** to display it.

③ Click and drag the sliders to define the foreground color.

● Click the Background icon to define the background color. Click the Foreground icon to switch back.

● You can also select a color by clicking the color ramp. This can be faster than opening the Color Picker dialog box (see "Choose the Foreground and Background Colors").

USING THE SWATCHES PALETTE

You can select or store colors using the Swatches palette.

USING THE SWATCHES PALETTE

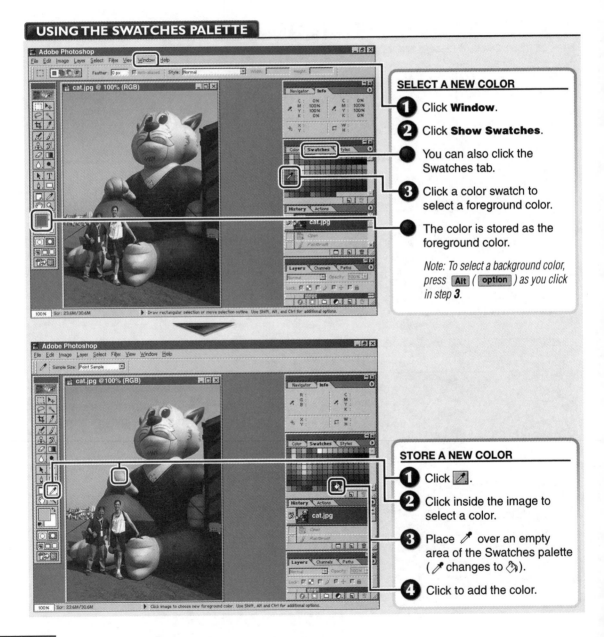

SELECT A NEW COLOR

1 Click **Window**.

2 Click **Show Swatches**.

● You can also click the Swatches tab.

3 Click a color swatch to select a foreground color.

● The color is stored as the foreground color.

Note: To select a background color, press [Alt] *(* [option] *) as you click in step 3.*

STORE A NEW COLOR

1 Click ✎.

2 Click inside the image to select a color.

3 Place ✎ over an empty area of the Swatches palette (✎ changes to ✋).

4 Click to add the color.

in an *instant*

The Color Swatch Name dialog box appears.

5 Type a name for the new color swatch.

6 Click **OK**.

The color is added as a new swatch.

To remove a swatch, press **Ctrl** (⌘) and place ✐ over a swatch (✐ changes to ✂). Click to delete the swatch.

RESET THE SWATCHES PALETTE

1 Click the Swatches ▶.

2 Click **Reset Swatches**.

SELECT A WEB-SAFE COLOR

Web-safe colors are guaranteed to display accurately in all Web browsers, no matter what type of color monitor a user has. You can select a Web-safe color with the Color Picker or Color palette.

SELECT A WEB-SAFE COLOR

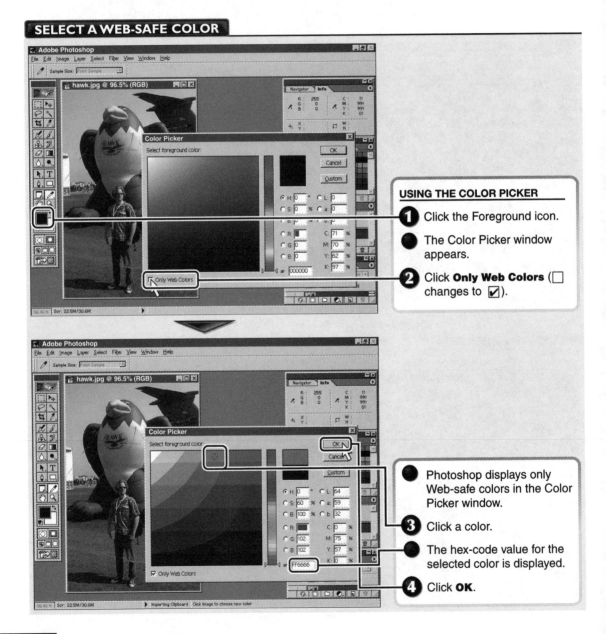

USING THE COLOR PICKER

1 Click the Foreground icon.

● The Color Picker window appears.

2 Click **Only Web Colors** (☐ changes to ☑).

● Photoshop displays only Web-safe colors in the Color Picker window.

3 Click a color.

● The hex-code value for the selected color is displayed.

4 Click **OK**.

in an *instant*

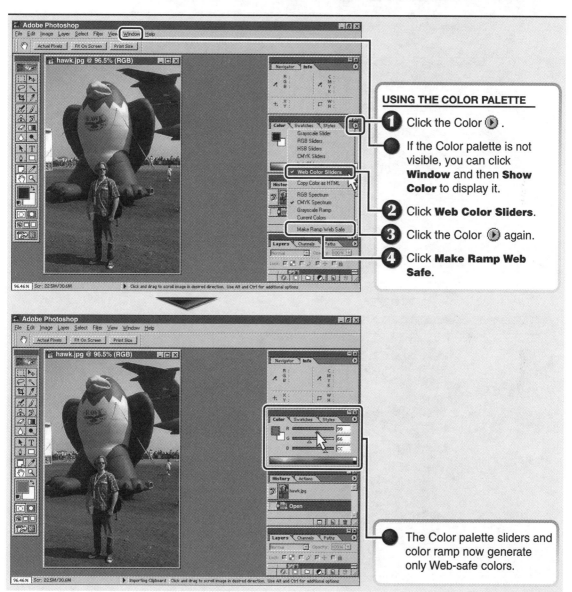

USING THE COLOR PALETTE

1 Click the Color ▶.

● If the Color palette is not visible, you can click **Window** and then **Show Color** to display it.

2 Click **Web Color Sliders**.

3 Click the Color ▶ again.

4 Click **Make Ramp Web Safe**.

● The Color palette sliders and color ramp now generate only Web-safe colors.

USING THE PAINTBRUSH TOOL

You can use the Paintbrush tool to add color to your image, just as if you were using an actual brush.

USING THE PAINTBRUSH TOOL

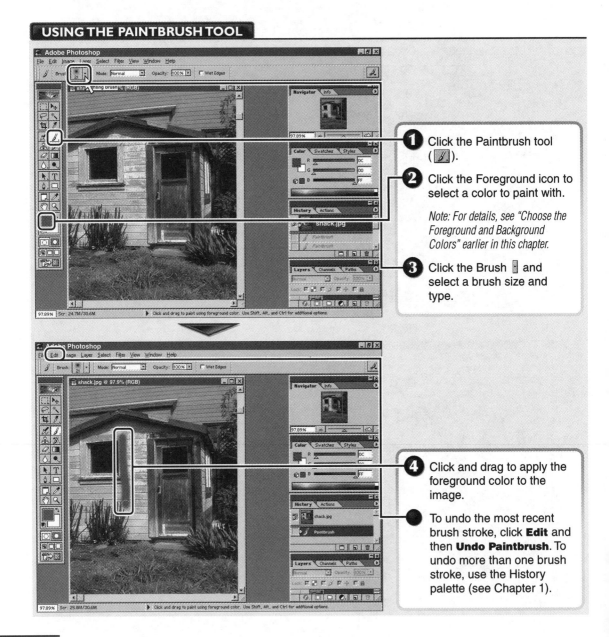

1 Click the Paintbrush tool ( ).

2 Click the Foreground icon to select a color to paint with.

Note: For details, see "Choose the Foreground and Background Colors" earlier in this chapter.

3 Click the Brush and select a brush size and type.

4 Click and drag to apply the foreground color to the image.

To undo the most recent brush stroke, click **Edit** and then **Undo Paintbrush**. To undo more than one brush stroke, use the History palette (see Chapter 1).

in an *instant*

5 Type a percentage value to change the opacity of the brush strokes.

● Alternatively, you can click the Opacity ▶ and adjust the slider.

6 Click and drag to apply the semitransparent paintbrush.

7 Click **Wet Edges** to concentrate the paint at the edges (☐ changes to ☑).

8 Click and drag to apply the customized paintbrush.

USING THE AIRBRUSH TOOL

You can use the Airbrush tool to add color to your image. The longer you click and hold with the Airbrush tool, the more color is applied.

USING THE AIRBRUSH TOOL

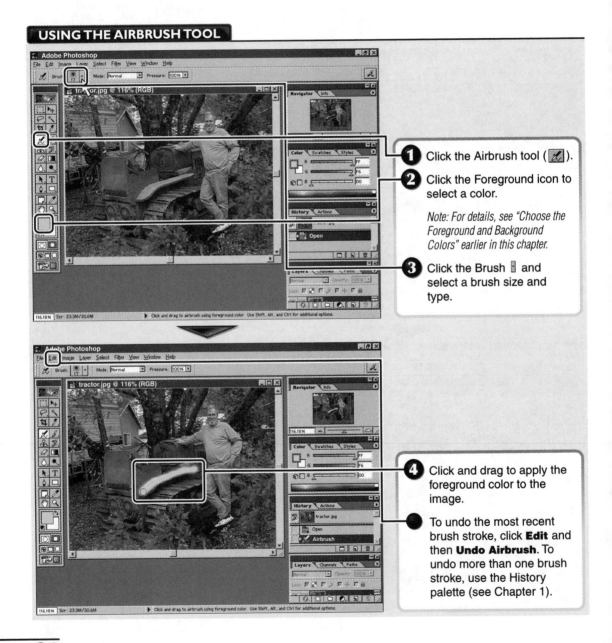

1 Click the Airbrush tool ( ).

2 Click the Foreground icon to select a color.

Note: For details, see "Choose the Foreground and Background Colors" earlier in this chapter.

3 Click the Brush ▪ and select a brush size and type.

4 Click and drag to apply the foreground color to the image.

To undo the most recent brush stroke, click **Edit** and then **Undo Airbrush**. To undo more than one brush stroke, use the History palette (see Chapter 1).

in an *instant*

5 Type a percentage value in the Pressure field to change the opacity of the brush strokes.

● Alternatively, you can click the Pressure ▸ and adjust the slider.

6 Click and drag to apply the semitransparent airbrush.

7 Click the Brush ▓ and select a speckled brush type.

8 Click and drag to create a rougher effect.

CHANGE BRUSH STYLES

You can change the style of your brushes by loading premade styles or creating a custom style from scratch. This gives you creative flexibility when working with your images.

CHANGE BRUSH STYLES

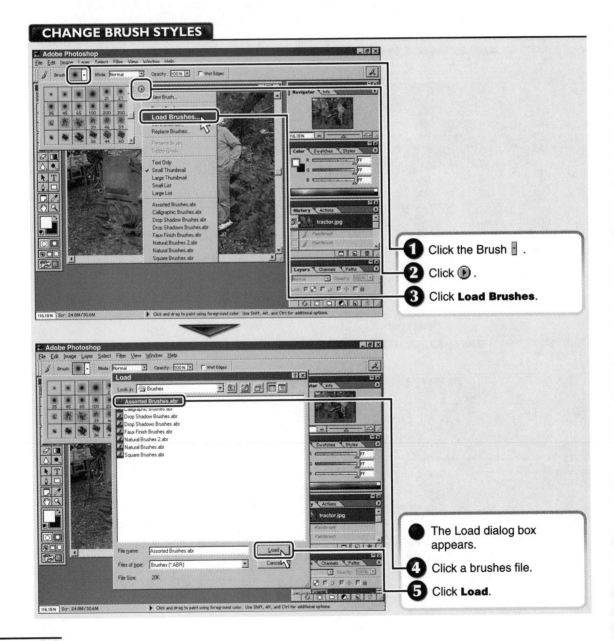

1 Click the Brush ▯ .

2 Click ⊙ .

3 Click **Load Brushes**.

● The Load dialog box appears.

4 Click a brushes file.

5 Click **Load**.

in an *instant*

6 Click the Brush **⬚**.

7 Click a brush size and type.

Note: Loaded brush styles are listed after existing brush styles.

8 Click to apply the brush inside the image.

● In this example, the brush was applied in single clicks (instead of clicking and dragging).

99

USING THE PAINT BUCKET TOOL

You can quickly fill in areas in your image with solid colors by using the Paint Bucket tool.

USING THE PAINT BUCKET TOOL

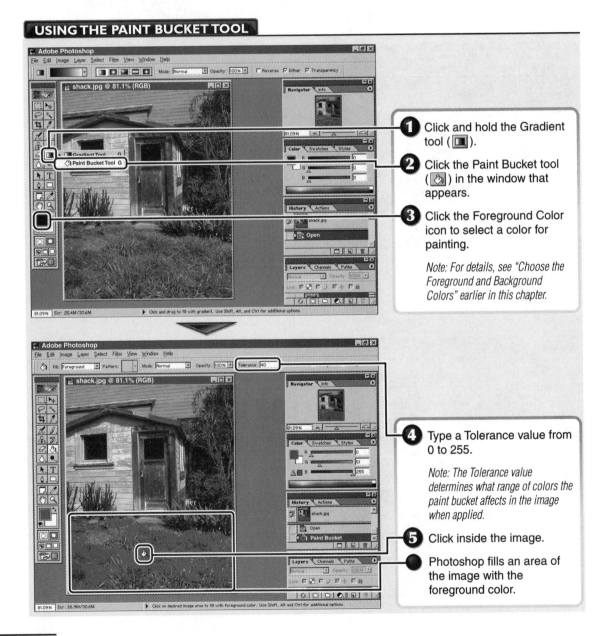

1 Click and hold the Gradient tool (⬛).

2 Click the Paint Bucket tool (🪣) in the window that appears.

3 Click the Foreground Color icon to select a color for painting.

Note: For details, see "Choose the Foreground and Background Colors" earlier in this chapter.

4 Type a Tolerance value from 0 to 255.

Note: The Tolerance value determines what range of colors the paint bucket affects in the image when applied.

5 Click inside the image.

■ Photoshop fills an area of the image with the foreground color.

in an instant

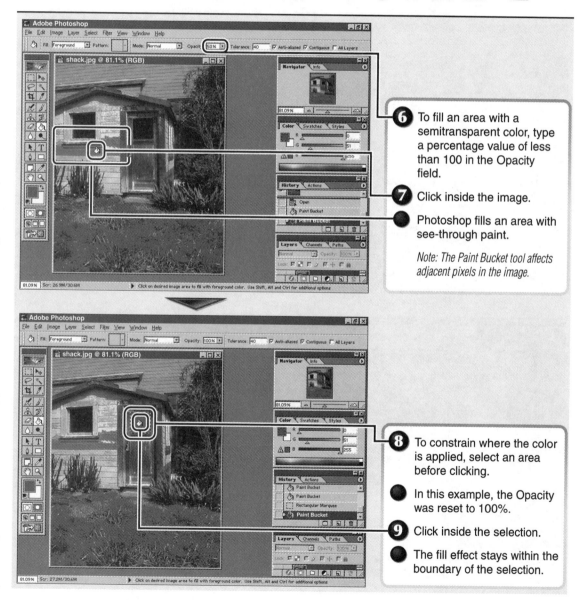

6 To fill an area with a semitransparent color, type a percentage value of less than 100 in the Opacity field.

7 Click inside the image.

● Photoshop fills an area with see-through paint.

Note: The Paint Bucket tool affects adjacent pixels in the image.

8 To constrain where the color is applied, select an area before clicking.

● In this example, the Opacity was reset to 100%.

9 Click inside the selection.

● The fill effect stays within the boundary of the selection.

FILL A SELECTION

You can fill a selection with the Fill command. The Fill command is an alternative to the Paint Bucket tool (see "Using the Paint Bucket Tool").

FILL A SELECTION

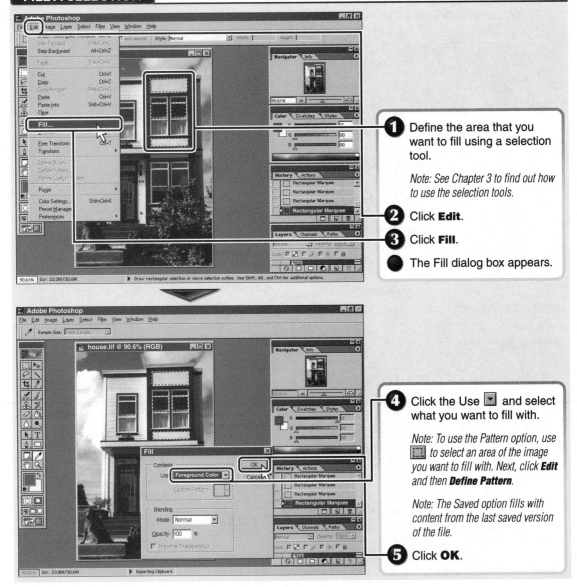

1 Define the area that you want to fill using a selection tool.

Note: See Chapter 3 to find out how to use the selection tools.

2 Click **Edit**.

3 Click **Fill**.

● The Fill dialog box appears.

4 Click the Use ▼ and select what you want to fill with.

*Note: To use the Pattern option, use [::] to select an area of the image you want to fill with. Next, click **Edit** and then **Define Pattern**.*

Note: The Saved option fills with content from the last saved version of the file.

5 Click **OK**.

in an *instant*

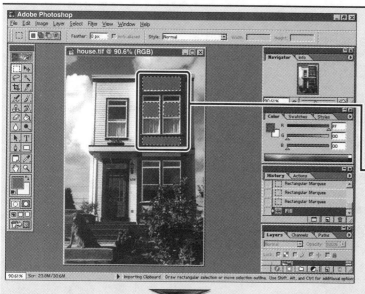

Photoshop fills the area.

*Note: The Fill command differs
from the Paint Bucket tool ( )
(see "Using the Paint Bucket Tool")
in that it fills the entire selected
area, not just adjacent pixels based
on a tolerance value.*

This is the Fill command
performed with the
background color instead.

DRAW SHAPES

You can create solid shapes in
your image by using
Photoshop's many shape tools.

DRAW SHAPES

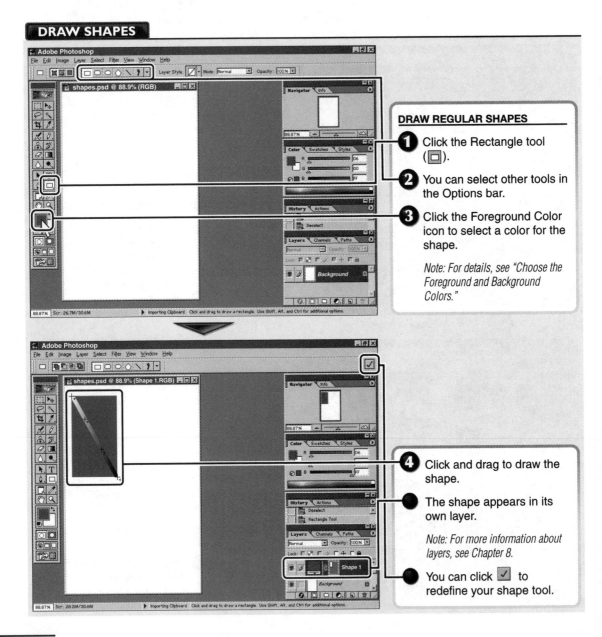

DRAW REGULAR SHAPES

1 Click the Rectangle tool
(▢).

2 You can select other tools in
the Options bar.

3 Click the Foreground Color
icon to select a color for the
shape.

*Note: For details, see "Choose the
Foreground and Background
Colors."*

4 Click and drag to draw the
shape.

● The shape appears in its
own layer.

*Note: For more information about
layers, see Chapter 8.*

● You can click ☑ to
redefine your shape tool.

in an *instant*

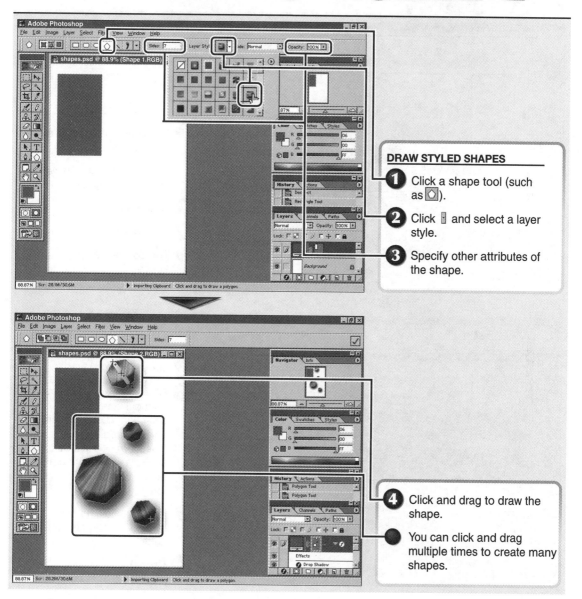

DRAW STYLED SHAPES

1 Click a shape tool (such as ⬠).

2 Click ▤ and select a layer style.

3 Specify other attributes of the shape.

4 Click and drag to draw the shape.

● You can click and drag multiple times to create many shapes.

STROKE A SELECTION

You can use the Stroke command to draw a line
along the edge of a selection.

STROKE A SELECTION

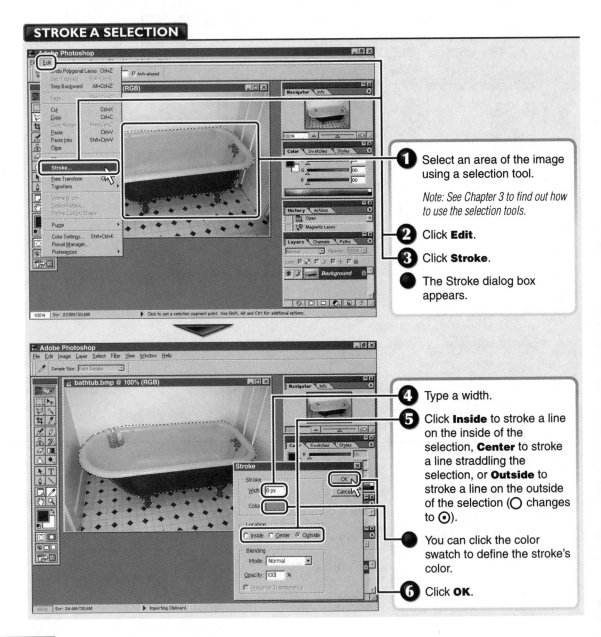

1 Select an area of the image
using a selection tool.

*Note: See Chapter 3 to find out how
to use the selection tools.*

2 Click **Edit**.

3 Click **Stroke**.

● The Stroke dialog box
appears.

4 Type a width.

5 Click **Inside** to stroke a line
on the inside of the
selection, **Center** to stroke
a line straddling the
selection, or **Outside** to
stroke a line on the outside
of the selection (○ changes
to ⊙).

● You can click the color
swatch to define the stroke's
color.

6 Click **OK**.

in an *instant*

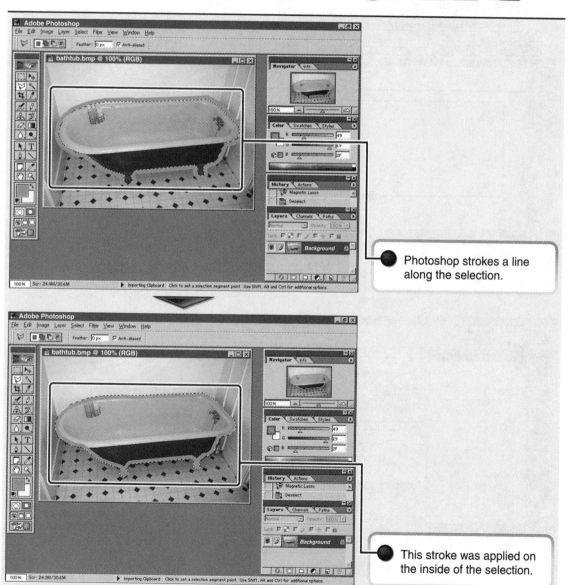

Photoshop strokes a line along the selection.

This stroke was applied on the inside of the selection.

APPLY A GRADIENT

You can apply a color gradient, which is a
blend from one color to another.

APPLY A GRADIENT

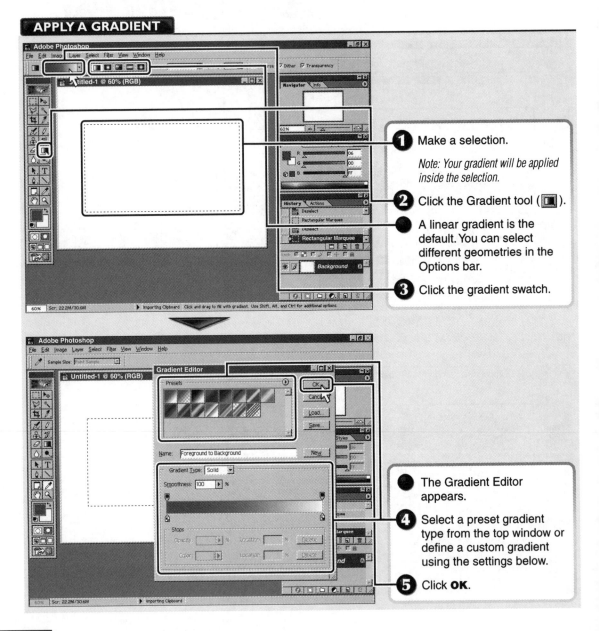

1 Make a selection.

*Note: Your gradient will be applied
inside the selection.*

2 Click the Gradient tool (▓).

A linear gradient is the
default. You can select
different geometries in the
Options bar.

3 Click the gradient swatch.

The Gradient Editor
appears.

4 Select a preset gradient
type from the top window or
define a custom gradient
using the settings below.

5 Click **OK**.

in an *instant*

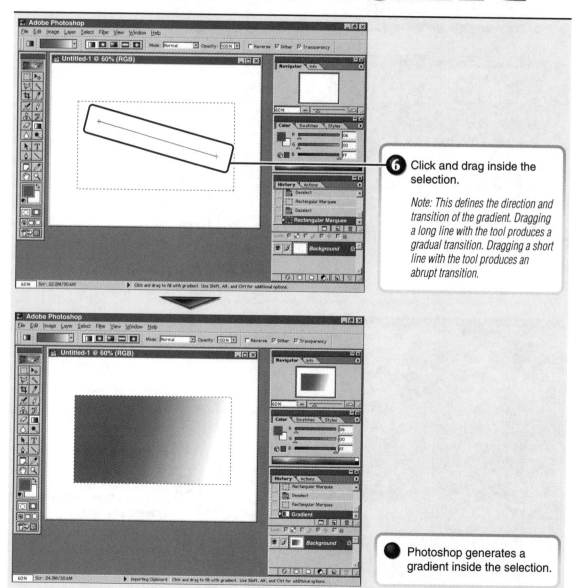

6 Click and drag inside the selection.

Note: This defines the direction and transition of the gradient. Dragging a long line with the tool produces a gradual transition. Dragging a short line with the tool produces an abrupt transition.

● Photoshop generates a gradient inside the selection.

USING THE HISTORY BRUSH

You can use the History brush to paint a previous state of your image from the History palette into the current image.

USING THE HISTORY BRUSH

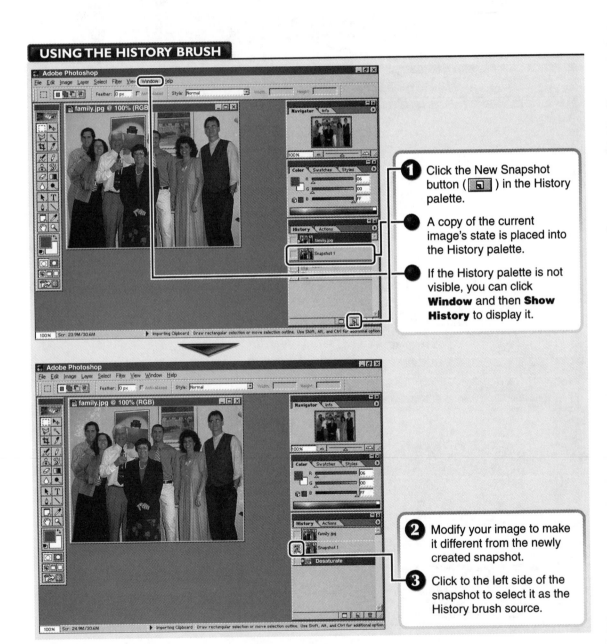

1 Click the New Snapshot button ( ) in the History palette.

● A copy of the current image's state is placed into the History palette.

● If the History palette is not visible, you can click **Window** and then **Show History** to display it.

2 Modify your image to make it different from the newly created snapshot.

3 Click to the left side of the snapshot to select it as the History brush source.

in an *instant*

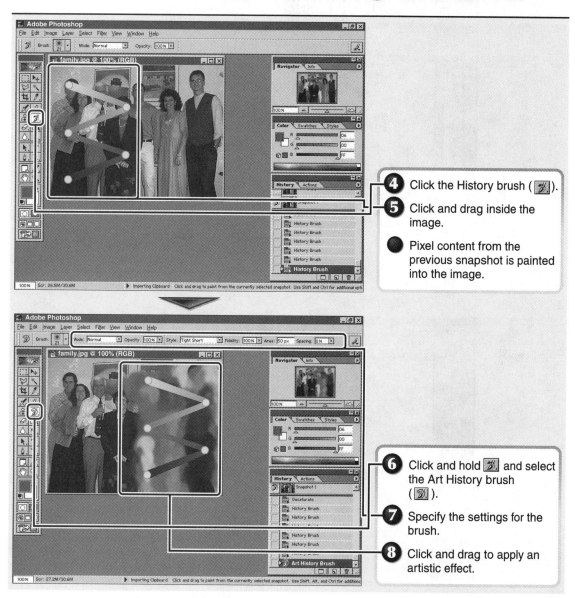

4 Click the History brush ( ).

5 Click and drag inside the image.

● Pixel content from the previous snapshot is painted into the image.

6 Click and hold and select the Art History brush ( ).

7 Specify the settings for the brush.

8 Click and drag to apply an artistic effect.

CHANGE BRIGHTNESS AND CONTRAST

The Brightness/Contrast command provides a simple way to make adjustments to the highlights and shadows of an entire image.

CHANGE BRIGHTNESS AND CONTRAST

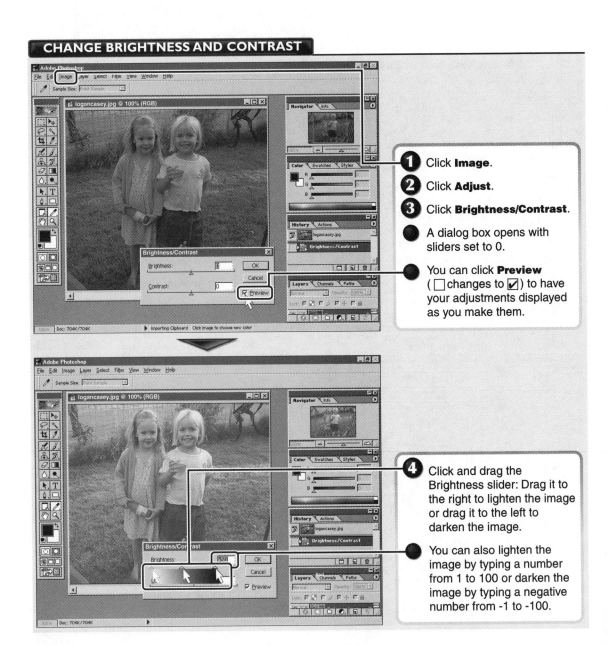

1 Click **Image**.

2 Click **Adjust**.

3 Click **Brightness/Contrast**.

■ A dialog box opens with sliders set to 0.

■ You can click **Preview** (☐ changes to ☑) to have your adjustments displayed as you make them.

4 Click and drag the Brightness slider: Drag it to the right to lighten the image or drag it to the left to darken the image.

■ You can also lighten the image by typing a number from 1 to 100 or darken the image by typing a negative number from -1 to -100.

in an *instant*

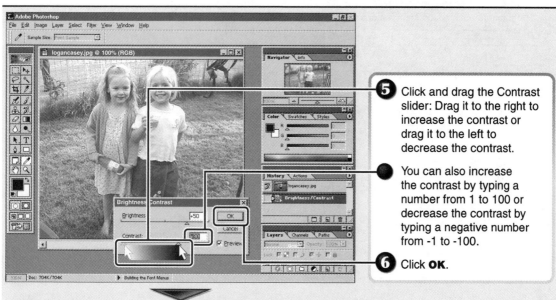

5 Click and drag the Contrast slider: Drag it to the right to increase the contrast or drag it to the left to decrease the contrast.

● You can also increase the contrast by typing a number from 1 to 100 or decrease the contrast by typing a negative number from -1 to -100.

6 Click **OK**.

● The new brightness and contrast values are applied.

Note: If you make a selection before performing the Brightness/Contrast command, only the selected pixels are affected. Similarly, if your image is multilayered, only the selected layer is affected.

USING THE DODGE AND BURN TOOLS

You can use the Dodge and Burn tools to brighten or darken a specific area of an image. These tools are an alternative to the Brightness/Contrast command, which affects an entire image.

USING THE DODGE TOOL

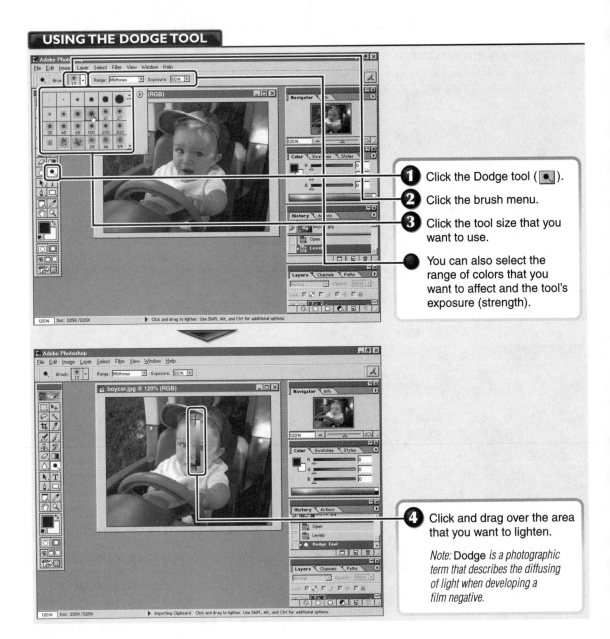

① Click the Dodge tool (🔦).

② Click the brush menu.

③ Click the tool size that you want to use.

● You can also select the range of colors that you want to affect and the tool's exposure (strength).

④ Click and drag over the area that you want to lighten.

Note: Dodge is a photographic term that describes the diffusing of light when developing a film negative.

in an *instant*

USING THE BURN TOOL

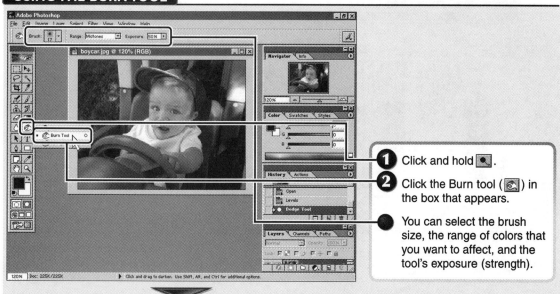

1 Click and hold [image].

2 Click the Burn tool ([image]) in the box that appears.

● You can select the brush size, the range of colors that you want to affect, and the tool's exposure (strength).

3 Click and drag over the area that you want to darken.

Note: Burn is a photographic term that describes the focusing of light when developing a film negative.

ADJUST IMAGE LEVELS

The Levels command enables you to make fine adjustments to the highlights, midtones, or shadows of an image. However, it is also more difficult to use than the Brightness/Contrast command.

ADJUST IMAGE LEVELS

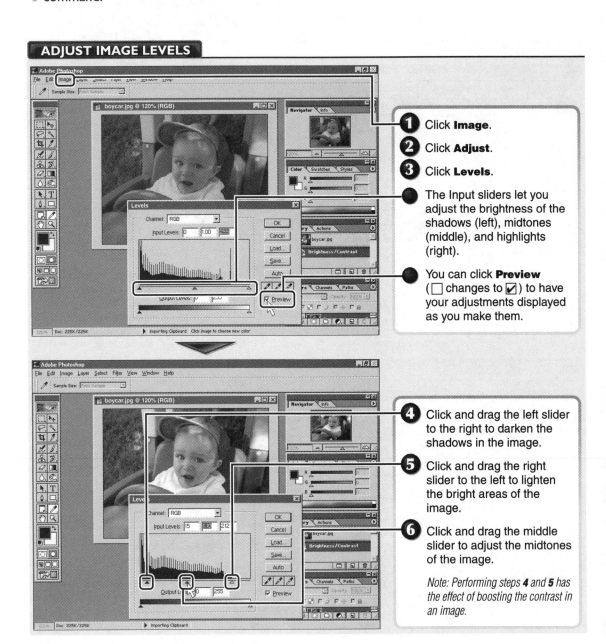

1 Click **Image**.

2 Click **Adjust**.

3 Click **Levels**.

The Input sliders let you adjust the brightness of the shadows (left), midtones (middle), and highlights (right).

You can click **Preview** (☐ changes to ☑) to have your adjustments displayed as you make them.

4 Click and drag the left slider to the right to darken the shadows in the image.

5 Click and drag the right slider to the left to lighten the bright areas of the image.

6 Click and drag the middle slider to adjust the midtones of the image.

*Note: Performing steps **4** and **5** has the effect of boosting the contrast in an image.*

in an *instant*

The Output sliders let you decrease the contrast while either lightening (using the left slider) or darkening (using the right slider) the image.

⑦ Click and drag the left slider to the right to darken the image.

⑧ Click and drag the right slider to the left to lighten the image.

⑨ Click **OK**.

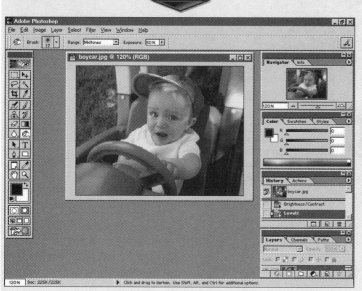

Photoshop makes brightness and contrast adjustments to the image.

Note: If you make a selection before performing the Levels command, only the selected pixels are affected. Similarly, if your image is multilayered, only the selected layer is affected.

ADJUST HUE AND SATURATION

You can change the hue to shift the component colors of an image. You can change the saturation to adjust the color intensity in an image.

ADJUST HUE AND SATURATION

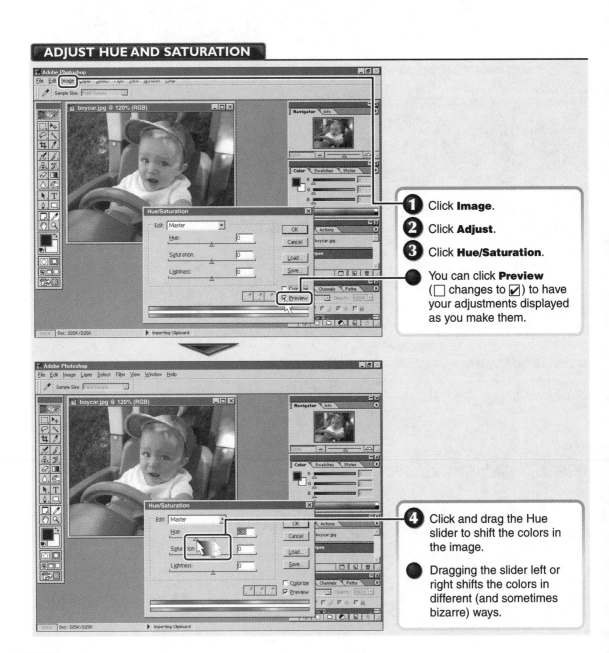

1 Click **Image**.

2 Click **Adjust**.

3 Click **Hue/Saturation**.

You can click **Preview** (☐ changes to ☑) to have your adjustments displayed as you make them.

4 Click and drag the Hue slider to shift the colors in the image.

Dragging the slider left or right shifts the colors in different (and sometimes bizarre) ways.

in an *instant*

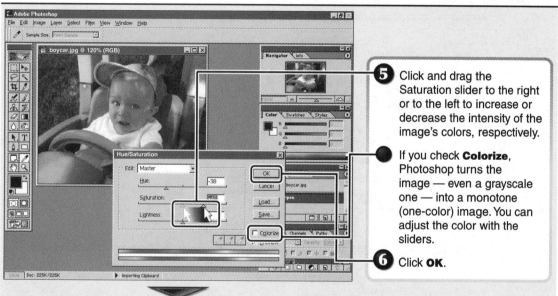

5 Click and drag the Saturation slider to the right or to the left to increase or decrease the intensity of the image's colors, respectively.

If you check **Colorize**, Photoshop turns the image — even a grayscale one — into a monotone (one-color) image. You can adjust the color with the sliders.

6 Click **OK**.

Photoshop makes the color adjustments to the image.

Note: If you make a selection before performing the Hue/Saturation command, only the selected pixels are affected. Similarly, if your image is multilayered, only the selected layer is affected.

USING THE SPONGE TOOL

You can use the Sponge tool to adjust the color saturation (color intensity) of a specific area of an image.

USING THE SPONGE TOOL

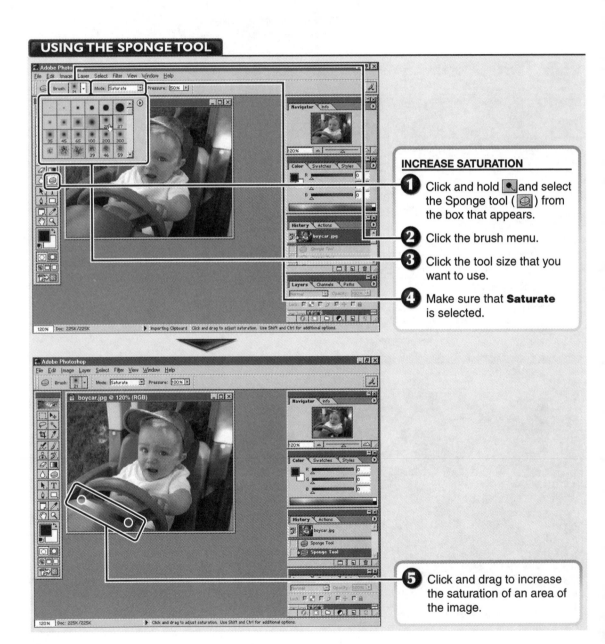

INCREASE SATURATION

1 Click and hold 🔍 and select the Sponge tool (🧽) from the box that appears.

2 Click the brush menu.

3 Click the tool size that you want to use.

4 Make sure that **Saturate** is selected.

5 Click and drag to increase the saturation of an area of the image.

in an **instant**

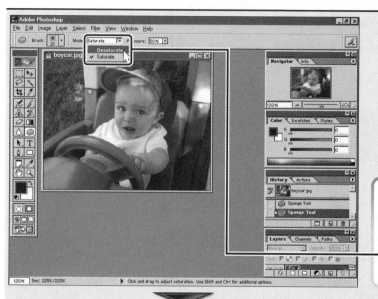

DECREASE SATURATION

1 Perform steps **1** through **3** earlier in this section.

2 Click ▾ and select **Desaturate**.

3 Click and drag to decrease the saturation of an area of the image.

● You can adjust the strength of the Sponge tool by changing the Pressure setting (from 1% to 100%).

ADJUST COLOR BALANCE

You can use the Color Balance command to change the amounts of specific colors in your image.

ADJUST COLOR BALANCE

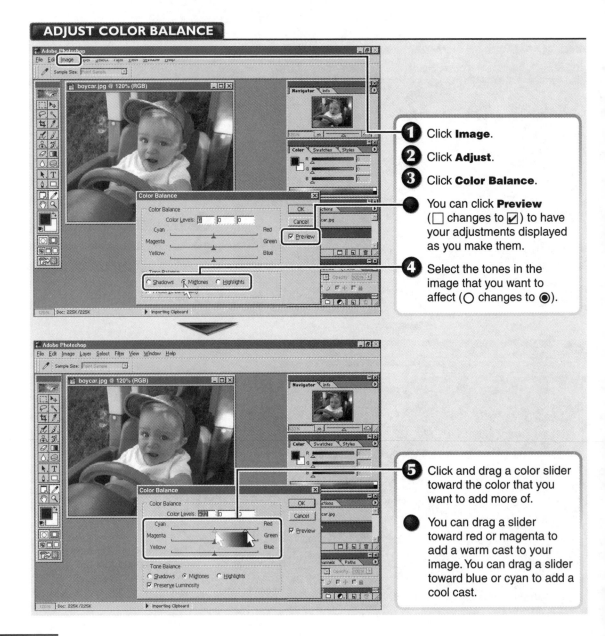

1 Click **Image**.

2 Click **Adjust**.

3 Click **Color Balance**.

■ You can click **Preview** (☐ changes to ☑) to have your adjustments displayed as you make them.

4 Select the tones in the image that you want to affect (○ changes to ◉).

5 Click and drag a color slider toward the color that you want to add more of.

■ You can drag a slider toward red or magenta to add a warm cast to your image. You can drag a slider toward blue or cyan to add a cool cast.

in an *instant*

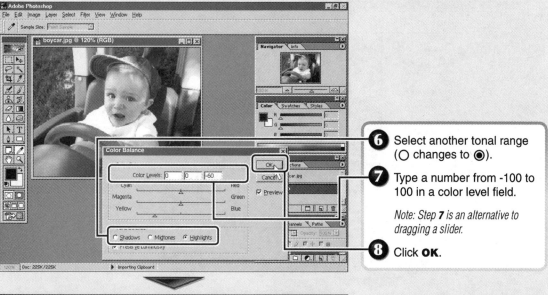

6 Select another tonal range
(○ changes to ◉).

7 Type a number from -100 to
100 in a color level field.

*Note: Step **7** is an alternative to
dragging a slider.*

8 Click **OK**.

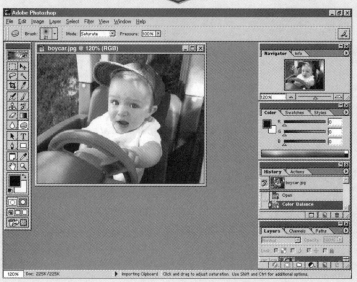

● Photoshop makes color
adjustments to the image.

*Note: If you make a selection before
performing the Color Balance
command, only the selected pixels
are affected. Similarly, if your image
is multilayered, only the selected
layer is affected.*

The Variations command gives you a user-friendly interface with which to perform color adjustments in your image.

USING THE VARIATIONS COMMAND

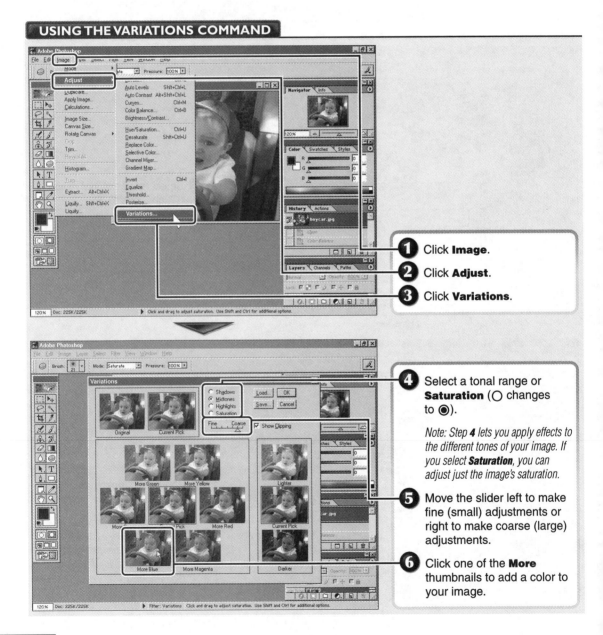

1 Click **Image**.

2 Click **Adjust**.

3 Click **Variations**.

4 Select a tonal range or **Saturation** (○ changes to ◉).

*Note: Step 4 lets you apply effects to the different tones of your image. If you select **Saturation**, you can adjust just the image's saturation.*

5 Move the slider left to make fine (small) adjustments or right to make coarse (large) adjustments.

6 Click one of the **More** thumbnails to add a color to your image.

in an *instant*

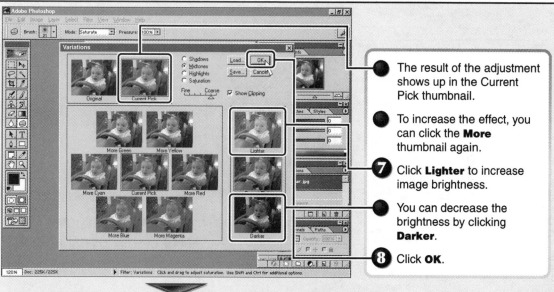

The result of the adjustment shows up in the Current Pick thumbnail.

To increase the effect, you can click the **More** thumbnail again.

7 Click **Lighter** to increase image brightness.

You can decrease the brightness by clicking **Darker**.

8 Click **OK**.

Photoshop makes the color adjustments to the image.

Note: If you make a selection before performing the Variations command, only the selected pixels are affected. Similarly, if your image is multilayered, only the selected layer is affected.

APPLY THE BLUR AND SHARPEN TOOLS

You can blur or sharpen specific areas of your image with the Blur and Sharpen tools.

APPLY THE BLUR TOOL

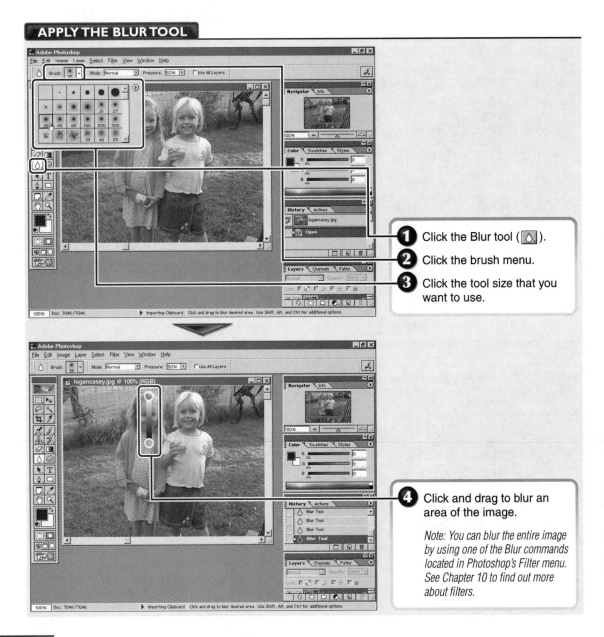

1 Click the Blur tool ( ).

2 Click the brush menu.

3 Click the tool size that you want to use.

4 Click and drag to blur an area of the image.

Note: You can blur the entire image by using one of the Blur commands located in Photoshop's Filter menu. See Chapter 10 to find out more about filters.

in an

APPLY THE SHARPEN TOOL

① Click and hold  and select the Sharpen tool ( ) from the box that appears.

② Enter a value from 1% to 100% to change the tool pressure (strength).

③ Click and drag to sharpen an area of the image.

Note: You can sharpen the entire image by using one of the Sharpen commands located in Photoshop's Filter menu. See Chapter 10 to find out more about filters.

CREATE AND ADD TO A LAYER

You can use layers to keep elements in your image independent
from one another. This gives you the ability to change one
element without disturbing others in your image.

CREATE A LAYER

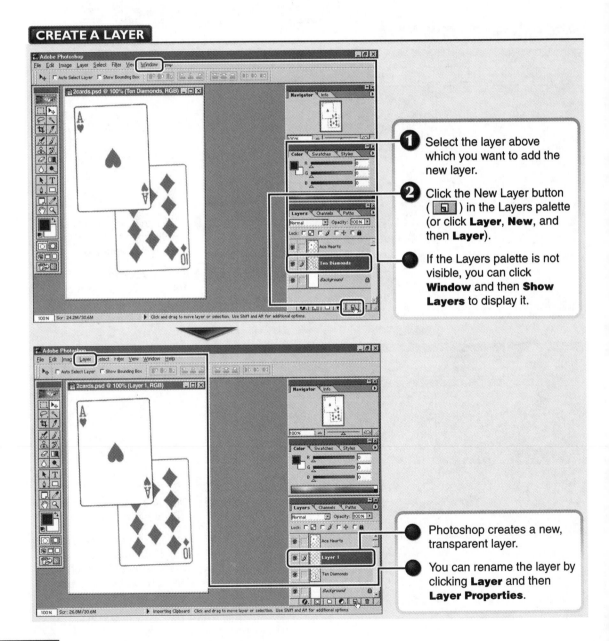

1 Select the layer above
which you want to add the
new layer.

2 Click the New Layer button
(▨) in the Layers palette
(or click **Layer**, **New**, and
then **Layer**).

● If the Layers palette is not
visible, you can click
Window and then **Show
Layers** to display it.

● Photoshop creates a new,
transparent layer.

● You can rename the layer by
clicking **Layer** and then
Layer Properties.

in an *instant*

ADD TO A LAYER

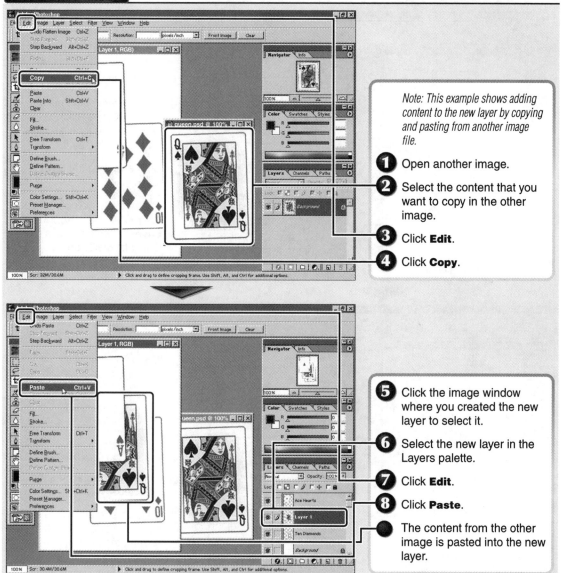

Note: This example shows adding content to the new layer by copying and pasting from another image file.

1 Open another image.

2 Select the content that you want to copy in the other image.

3 Click **Edit**.

4 Click **Copy**.

5 Click the image window where you created the new layer to select it.

6 Select the new layer in the Layers palette.

7 Click **Edit**.

8 Click **Paste**.

● The content from the other image is pasted into the new layer.

DUPLICATE OR MOVE A LAYER

By duplicating a layer, you can manipulate elements in an image while keeping a copy of their original state. You can use the Move tool to reposition the elements in one layer without moving those in others.

DUPLICATE A LAYER

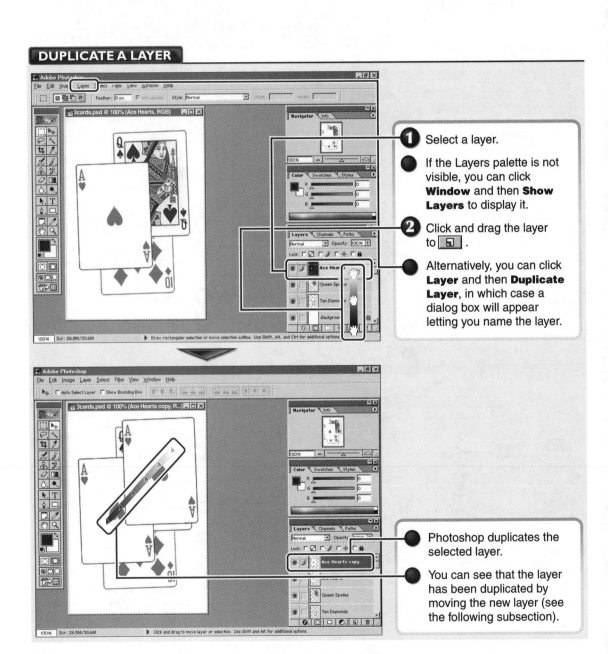

1 Select a layer.

■ If the Layers palette is not visible, you can click **Window** and then **Show Layers** to display it.

2 Click and drag the layer to 🔲 .

■ Alternatively, you can click **Layer** and then **Duplicate Layer**, in which case a dialog box will appear letting you name the layer.

■ Photoshop duplicates the selected layer.

■ You can see that the layer has been duplicated by moving the new layer (see the following subsection).

in an instant

MOVE A LAYER

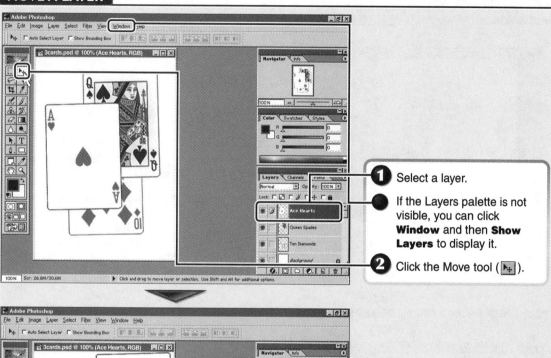

1 Select a layer.

● If the Layers palette is not visible, you can click **Window** and then **Show Layers** to display it.

2 Click the Move tool (🕂).

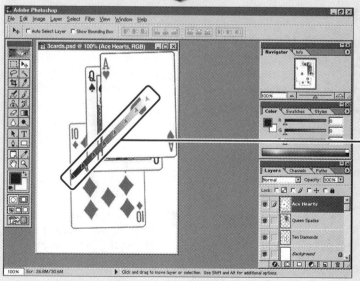

3 Click and drag inside the window.

● Content in the selected layer moves. Content in the other layers remains in the same location.

Note: To move several layers at once, see "Link and Move Multiple Layers."

HIDE OR DELETE A LAYER

You can hide a layer to temporarily remove elements in that layer from view. You can delete a layer when you no longer have a use for its contents.

HIDE A LAYER

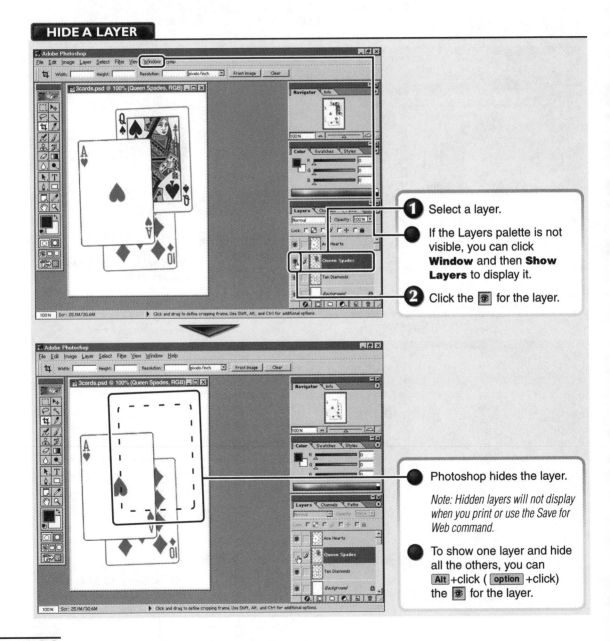

1 Select a layer.

■ If the Layers palette is not visible, you can click **Window** and then **Show Layers** to display it.

2 Click the 👁 for the layer.

■ Photoshop hides the layer.

Note: Hidden layers will not display when you print or use the Save for Web command.

■ To show one layer and hide all the others, you can **Alt** +click (**option** +click) the 👁 for the layer.

in an *instant*

DELETE A LAYER

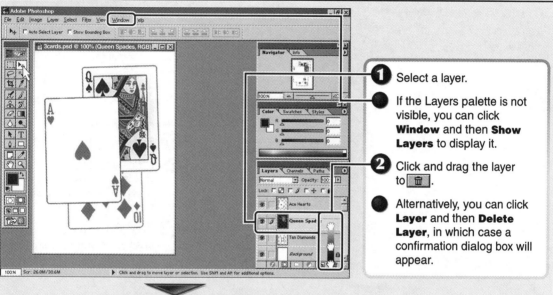

1 Select a layer.

● If the Layers palette is not visible, you can click **Window** and then **Show Layers** to display it.

2 Click and drag the layer to 🗑.

● Alternatively, you can click **Layer** and then **Delete Layer**, in which case a confirmation dialog box will appear.

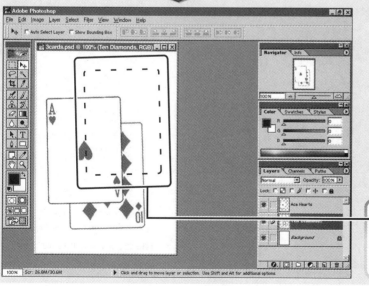

● Photoshop deletes the selected layer. The content in the layer disappears from the image window.

REORDER LAYERS

You can reorder layers to move elements forward or backward in your image by using the Layers palette or the Arrange commands.

USING THE LAYERS PALETTE

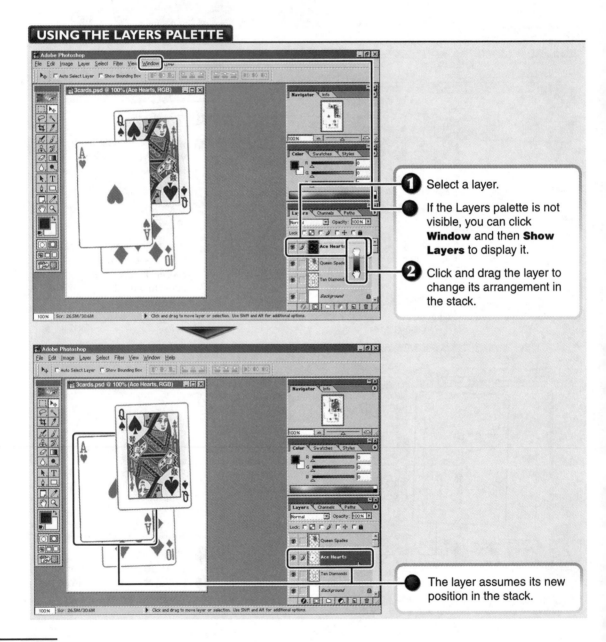

1 Select a layer.

■ If the Layers palette is not visible, you can click **Window** and then **Show Layers** to display it.

2 Click and drag the layer to change its arrangement in the stack.

■ The layer assumes its new position in the stack.

in an *instant*

USING THE ARRANGE COMMAND

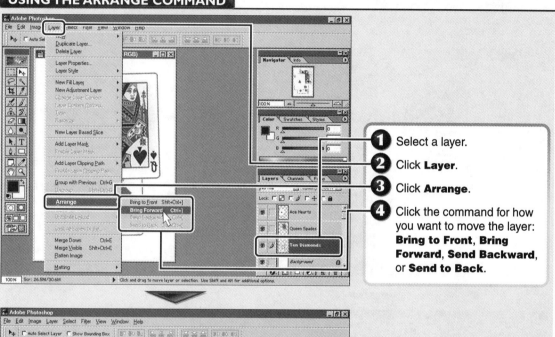

1 Select a layer.

2 Click **Layer**.

3 Click **Arrange**.

4 Click the command for how you want to move the layer: **Bring to Front**, **Bring Forward**, **Send Backward**, or **Send to Back**.

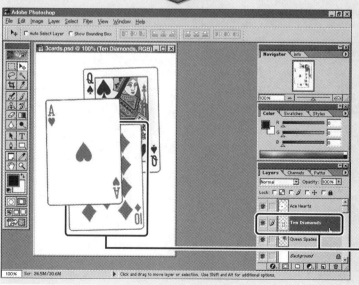

● The layer assumes its new position in the stack.

CHANGE LAYER OPACITY

Adjusting the opacity of a layer lets elements in the layers below it show through. The more opaque a layer is, the less you can see the layers below it.

CHANGE LAYER OPACITY

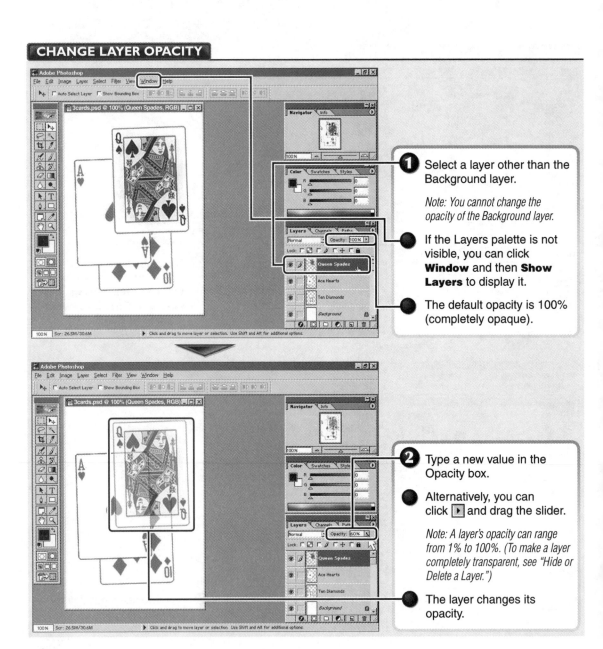

1 Select a layer other than the Background layer.

Note: You cannot change the opacity of the Background layer.

If the Layers palette is not visible, you can click **Window** and then **Show Layers** to display it.

The default opacity is 100% (completely opaque).

2 Type a new value in the Opacity box.

Alternatively, you can click ▶ and drag the slider.

Note: A layer's opacity can range from 1% to 100%. (To make a layer completely transparent, see "Hide or Delete a Layer.")

The layer changes its opacity.

in an instant

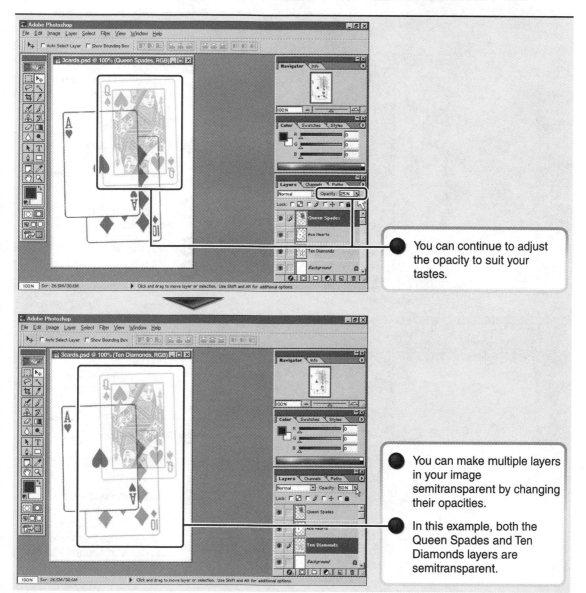

You can continue to adjust the opacity to suit your tastes.

You can make multiple layers in your image semitransparent by changing their opacities.

In this example, both the Queen Spades and Ten Diamonds layers are semitransparent.

MERGE AND FLATTEN LAYERS

Merging layers lets you combine information from two or more separate layers. Flattening layers combines all the layers of an image into one.

MERGE TWO LAYERS

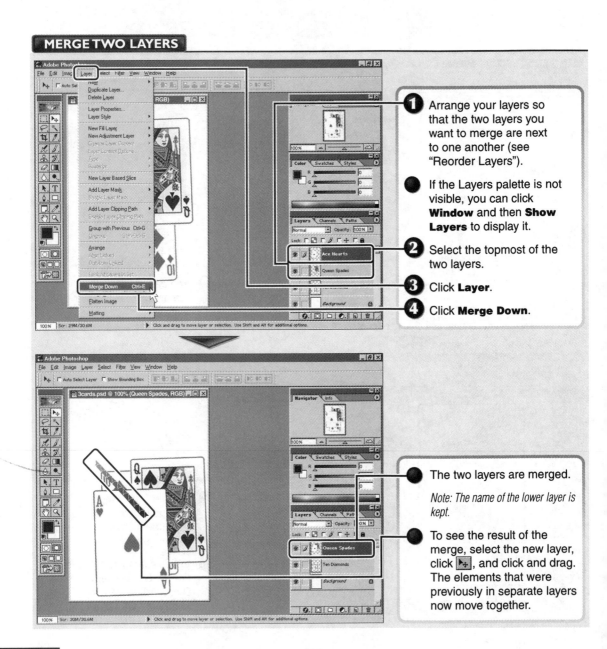

1 Arrange your layers so that the two layers you want to merge are next to one another (see "Reorder Layers").

● If the Layers palette is not visible, you can click **Window** and then **Show Layers** to display it.

2 Select the topmost of the two layers.

3 Click **Layer**.

4 Click **Merge Down**.

● The two layers are merged.

Note: The name of the lower layer is kept.

● To see the result of the merge, select the new layer, click , and click and drag. The elements that were previously in separate layers now move together.

in an *instant*

FLATTEN AN IMAGE

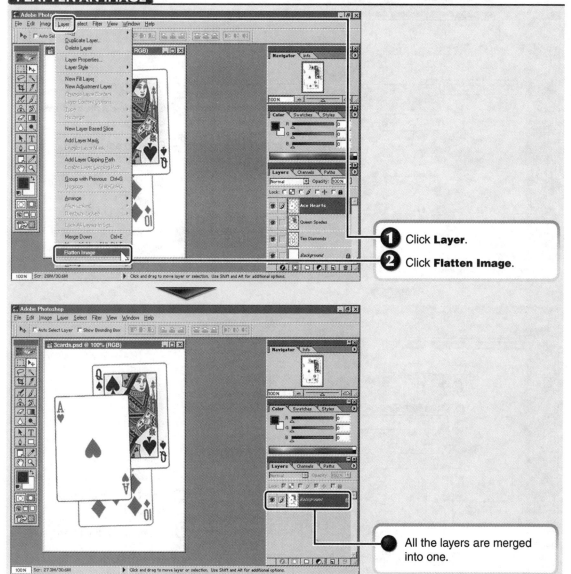

1 Click **Layer**.

2 Click **Flatten Image**.

All the layers are merged into one.

CREATE AN ADJUSTMENT LAYER

Adjustment layers let you store color and tonal changes in a layer rather than have them permanently applied to your image.

CREATE AN ADJUSTMENT LAYER

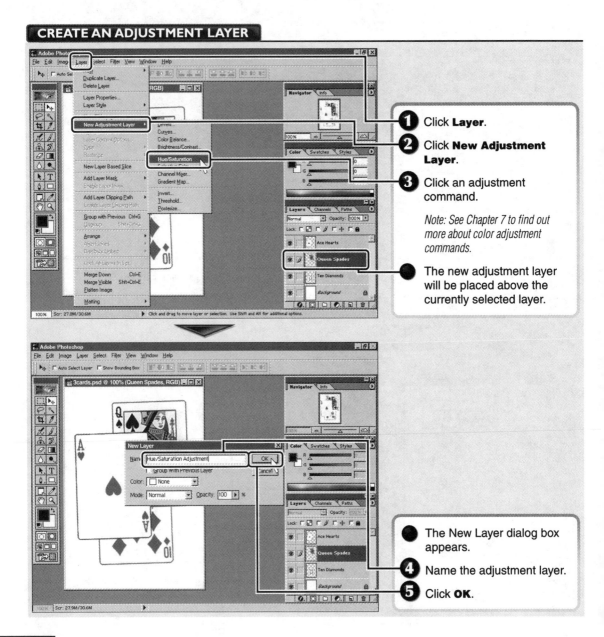

1 Click **Layer**.

2 Click **New Adjustment Layer**.

3 Click an adjustment command.

Note: See Chapter 7 to find out more about color adjustment commands.

● The new adjustment layer will be placed above the currently selected layer.

● The New Layer dialog box appears.

4 Name the adjustment layer.

5 Click **OK**.

in an instant

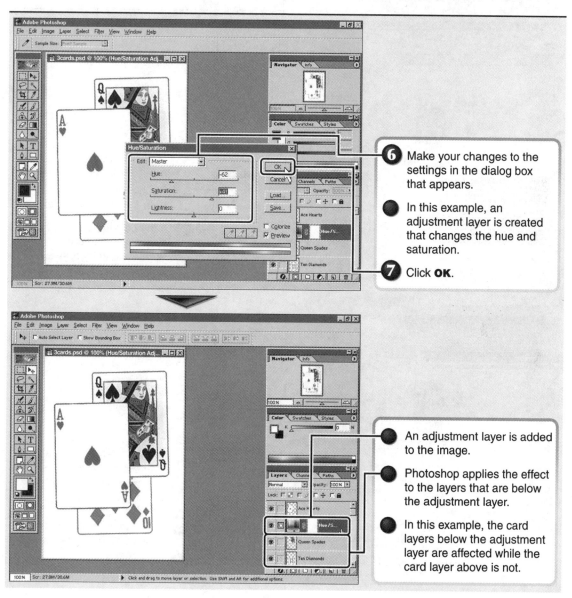

6 Make your changes to the settings in the dialog box that appears.

● In this example, an adjustment layer is created that changes the hue and saturation.

7 Click **OK**.

● An adjustment layer is added to the image.

● Photoshop applies the effect to the layers that are below the adjustment layer.

● In this example, the card layers below the adjustment layer are affected while the card layer above is not.

EDIT AN ADJUSTMENT LAYER

You can change the color and tonal changes that you defined in an adjustment layer.

EDIT AN ADJUSTMENT LAYER

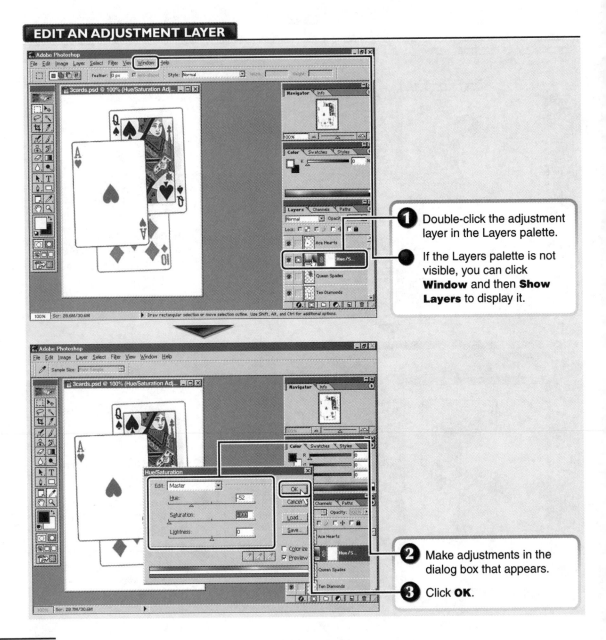

1 Double-click the adjustment layer in the Layers palette.

If the Layers palette is not visible, you can click **Window** and then **Show Layers** to display it.

2 Make adjustments in the dialog box that appears.

3 Click **OK**.

in an instant

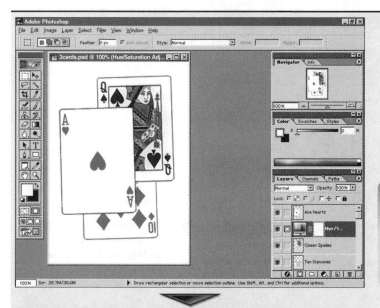

In this example, the saturation was reduced to the minimum, which removed the color in the layers below the adjustment layer.

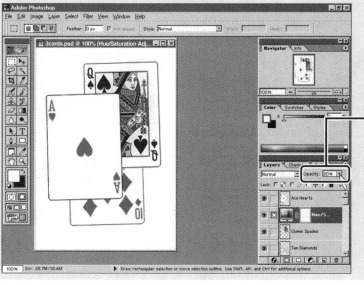

4 To lessen the affect of an adjustment layer, decrease the layer's opacity to less than 100%.

In this example, the opacity was decreased to 20%, which reverses the decrease in saturation. Some of the original color in the cards returns.

LINK AND MOVE MULTIPLE LAYERS

Linking causes different layers to move in unison when using the Move tool. Linking is useful when you want to keep elements of an image aligned with one another, but do not want to merge their layers.

LINK LAYERS

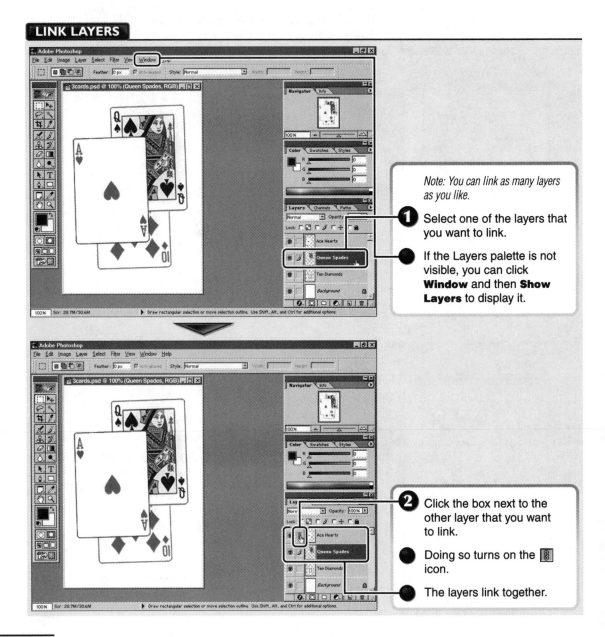

Note: You can link as many layers as you like.

1 Select one of the layers that you want to link.

● If the Layers palette is not visible, you can click **Window** and then **Show Layers** to display it.

2 Click the box next to the other layer that you want to link.

● Doing so turns on the 🔗 icon.

● The layers link together.

in an *instant*

MOVE MULTIPLE LAYERS

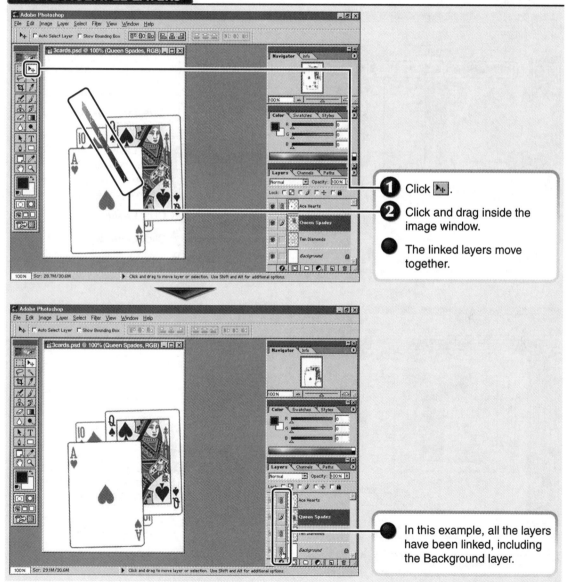

1 Click ▶+.

2 Click and drag inside the image window.

● The linked layers move together.

● In this example, all the layers have been linked, including the Background layer.

BLEND LAYERS

You can use Photoshop's blending modes to specify how pixels in a layer are blended with the layers below it.

BLEND LAYERS

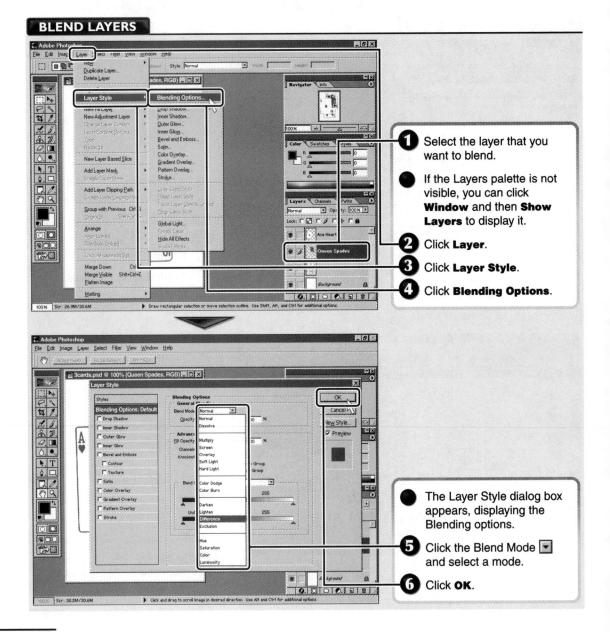

1 Select the layer that you want to blend.

● If the Layers palette is not visible, you can click **Window** and then **Show Layers** to display it.

2 Click **Layer**.

3 Click **Layer Style**.

4 Click **Blending Options**.

● The Layer Style dialog box appears, displaying the Blending options.

5 Click the Blend Mode ▾ and select a mode.

6 Click **OK**.

in an *instant*

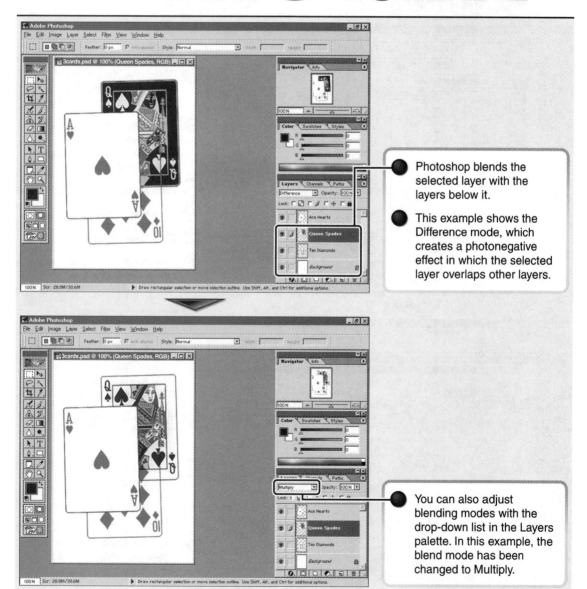

Photoshop blends the selected layer with the layers below it.

This example shows the Difference mode, which creates a photonegative effect in which the selected layer overlaps other layers.

You can also adjust blending modes with the drop-down list in the Layers palette. In this example, the blend mode has been changed to Multiply.

You can apply a drop shadow to make a layer look like it is raised off the image canvas.

APPLY A DROP SHADOW

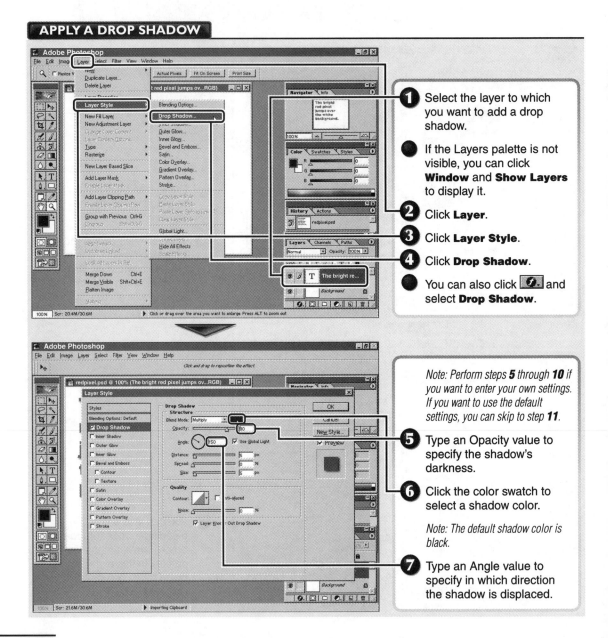

1 Select the layer to which you want to add a drop shadow.

● If the Layers palette is not visible, you can click **Window** and **Show Layers** to display it.

2 Click **Layer**.

3 Click **Layer Style**.

4 Click **Drop Shadow**.

● You can also click and select **Drop Shadow**.

Note: Perform steps **5** through **10** if you want to enter your own settings. If you want to use the default settings, you can skip to step **11**.

5 Type an Opacity value to specify the shadow's darkness.

6 Click the color swatch to select a shadow color.

Note: The default shadow color is black.

7 Type an Angle value to specify in which direction the shadow is displaced.

148

in an *instant*

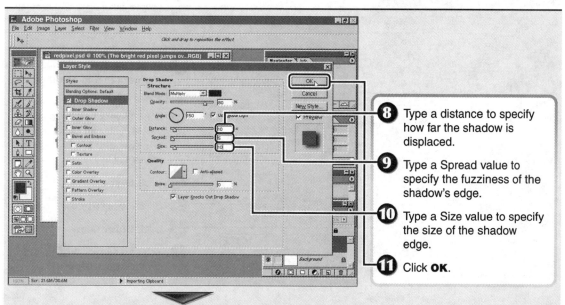

8 Type a distance to specify how far the shadow is displaced.

9 Type a Spread value to specify the fuzziness of the shadow's edge.

10 Type a Size value to specify the size of the shadow edge.

11 Click **OK**.

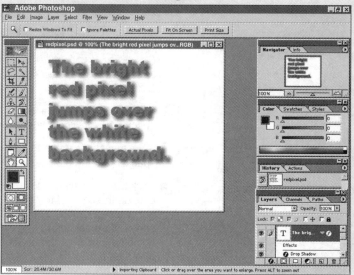

● Photoshop creates a shadow in back of the selected layer.

Note: In this example, the effect was applied to a layer of type. To find out more about type, see Chapter 11.

APPLY AN OUTER GLOW

The outer glow effect adds faint coloring to the outside edge of a layer.

APPLY AN OUTER GLOW

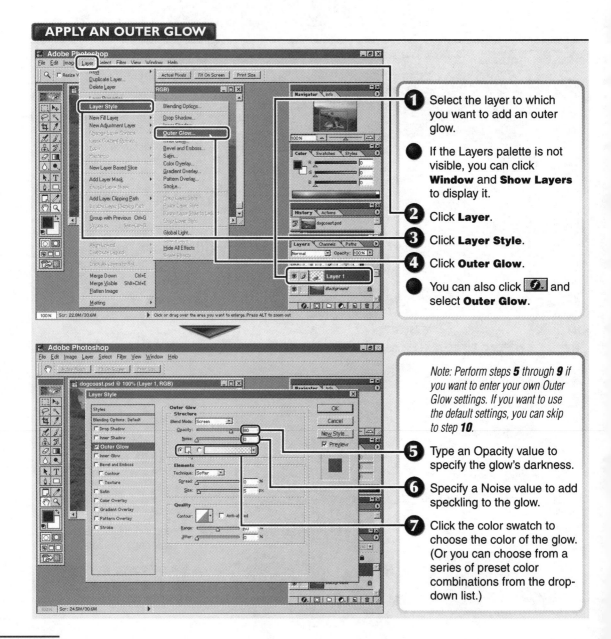

1 Select the layer to which you want to add an outer glow.

● If the Layers palette is not visible, you can click **Window** and **Show Layers** to display it.

2 Click **Layer**.

3 Click **Layer Style**.

4 Click **Outer Glow**.

● You can also click 🖉. and select **Outer Glow**.

Note: Perform steps 5 through 9 if you want to enter your own Outer Glow settings. If you want to use the default settings, you can skip to step 10.

5 Type an Opacity value to specify the glow's darkness.

6 Specify a Noise value to add speckling to the glow.

7 Click the color swatch to choose the color of the glow. (Or you can choose from a series of preset color combinations from the drop-down list.)

in an *instant*

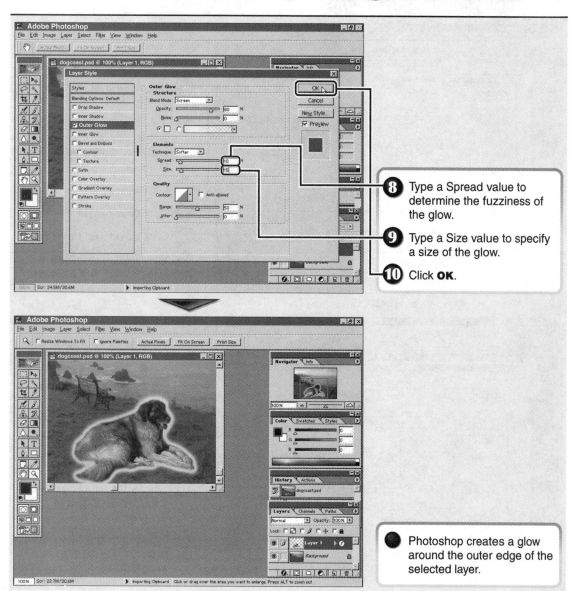

8 Type a Spread value to determine the fuzziness of the glow.

9 Type a Size value to specify a size of the glow.

10 Click **OK**.

● Photoshop creates a glow around the outer edge of the selected layer.

You can bevel and emboss a layer to give it
a three-dimensional look.

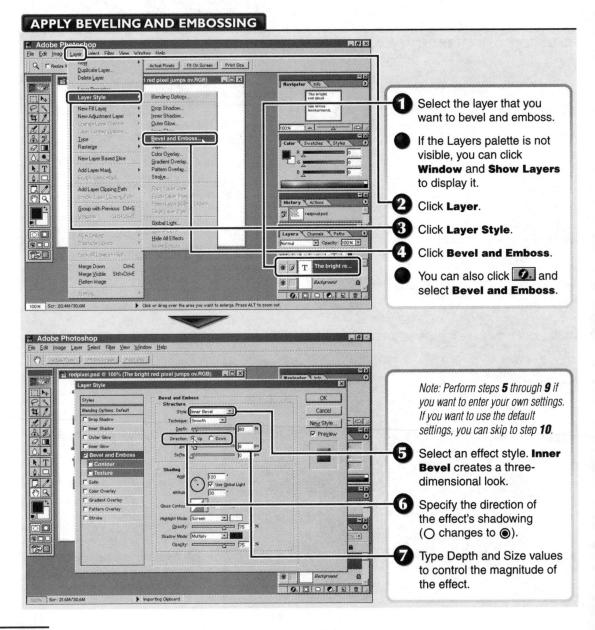

APPLY BEVELING AND EMBOSSING

1 Select the layer that you
want to bevel and emboss.

● If the Layers palette is not
visible, you can click
Window and **Show Layers**
to display it.

2 Click **Layer**.

3 Click **Layer Style**.

4 Click **Bevel and Emboss**.

● You can also click ⬛ and
select **Bevel and Emboss**.

*Note: Perform steps **5** through **9** if
you want to enter your own settings.
If you want to use the default
settings, you can skip to step **10**.*

5 Select an effect style. **Inner
Bevel** creates a three-
dimensional look.

6 Specify the direction of
the effect's shadowing
(○ changes to ⬤).

7 Type Depth and Size values
to control the magnitude of
the effect.

in an instant

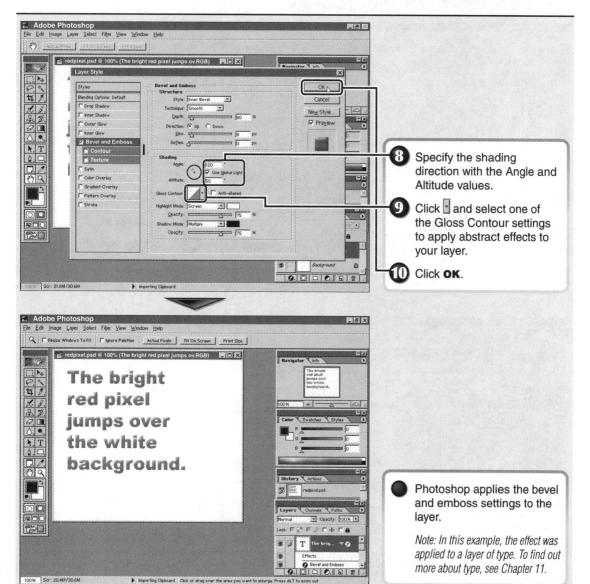

8 Specify the shading direction with the Angle and Altitude values.

9 Click ⬚ and select one of the Gloss Contour settings to apply abstract effects to your layer.

10 Click **OK**.

The bright red pixel jumps over the white background.

● Photoshop applies the bevel and emboss settings to the layer.

Note: In this example, the effect was applied to a layer of type. To find out more about type, see Chapter 11.

APPLY MULTIPLE EFFECTS TO A LAYER

You can apply multiple layer effects to layers in your image. This enables you to style your layers in complex ways.

APPLY MULTIPLE EFFECTS TO A LAYER

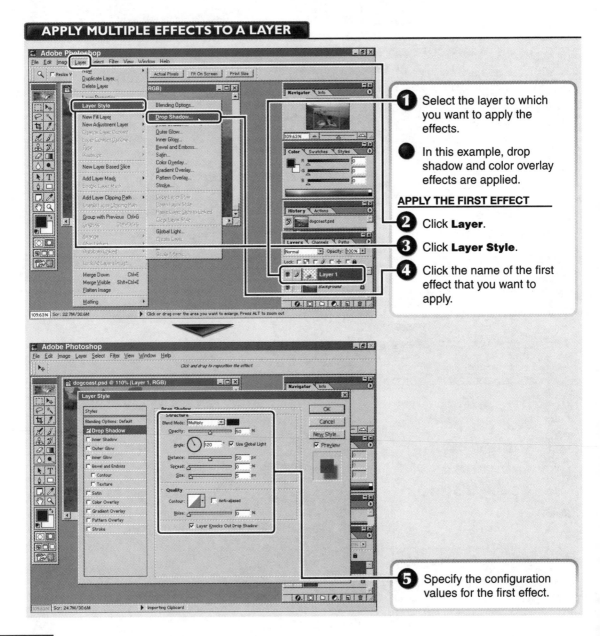

1 Select the layer to which you want to apply the effects.

● In this example, drop shadow and color overlay effects are applied.

APPLY THE FIRST EFFECT

2 Click **Layer**.

3 Click **Layer Style**.

4 Click the name of the first effect that you want to apply.

5 Specify the configuration values for the first effect.

in an *instant*

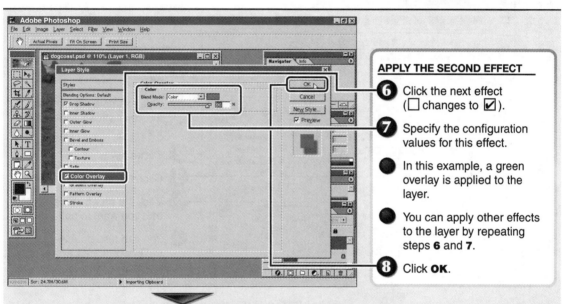

APPLY THE SECOND EFFECT

6 Click the next effect
(☐ changes to ☑).

7 Specify the configuration
values for this effect.

● In this example, a green
overlay is applied to the
layer.

● You can apply other effects
to the layer by repeating
steps **6** and **7**.

8 Click **OK**.

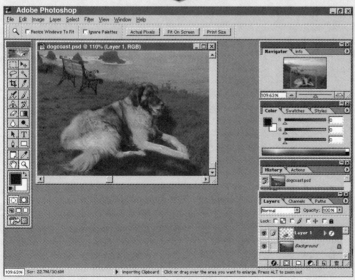

● Photoshop applies the
effects to the layer.

EDIT A LAYER EFFECT

You can edit a layer effect that you have applied to your image. This lets you fine-tune the effect to achieve an appearance that suits you.

EDIT A LAYER EFFECT

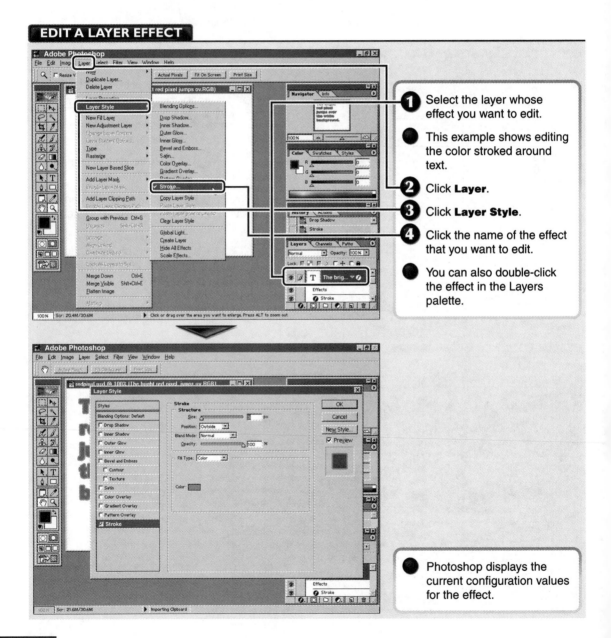

1 Select the layer whose effect you want to edit.

● This example shows editing the color stroked around text.

2 Click **Layer**.

3 Click **Layer Style**.

4 Click the name of the effect that you want to edit.

● You can also double-click the effect in the Layers palette.

● Photoshop displays the current configuration values for the effect.

in an *instant*

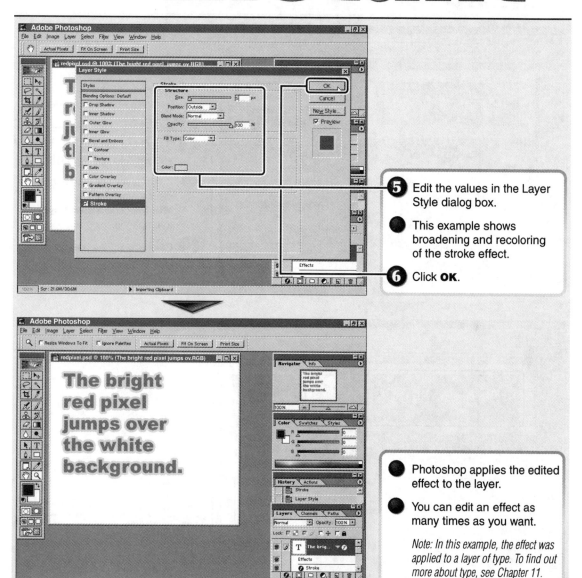

5 Edit the values in the Layer Style dialog box.

● This example shows broadening and recoloring of the stroke effect.

6 Click **OK**.

● Photoshop applies the edited effect to the layer.

● You can edit an effect as many times as you want.

Note: In this example, the effect was applied to a layer of type. To find out more about type, see Chapter 11.

APPLY STYLES

You can apply a Photoshop style to a layer to give the layer a colorful or textured look. Styles are predefined combinations of Photoshop effects (such as Drop Shadow and Outer Glow).

APPLY STYLES

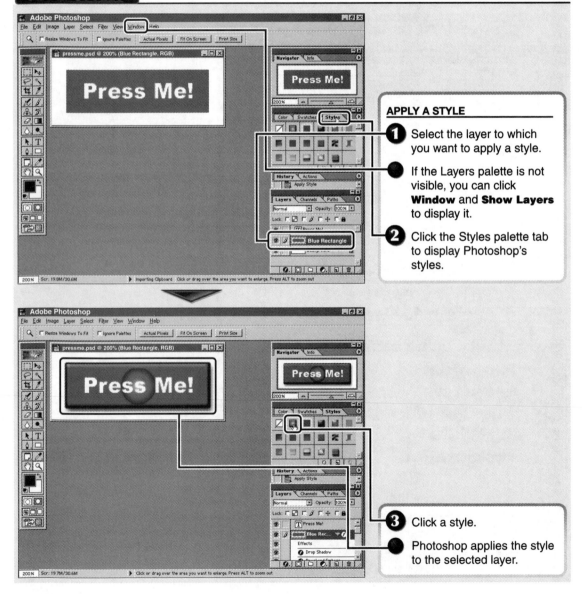

APPLY A STYLE

1 Select the layer to which you want to apply a style.

■ If the Layers palette is not visible, you can click **Window** and **Show Layers** to display it.

2 Click the Styles palette tab to display Photoshop's styles.

3 Click a style.

■ Photoshop applies the style to the selected layer.

in an *instant*

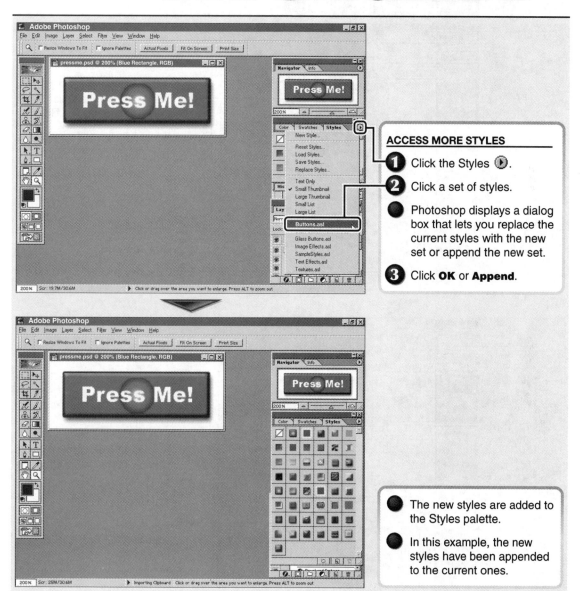

ACCESS MORE STYLES

1 Click the Styles ⊙.

2 Click a set of styles.

● Photoshop displays a dialog box that lets you replace the current styles with the new set or append the new set.

3 Click **OK** or **Append**.

● The new styles are added to the Styles palette.

● In this example, the new styles have been appended to the current ones.

APPLY AN ARTISTIC FILTER: DRY BRUSH

The Artistic filters make your image look as though it was created using traditional artistic techniques. The Dry Brush filter, for example, applies a painted effect by converting similarly colored areas in your image to solid colors.

APPLY AN ARTISTIC FILTER: DRY BRUSH

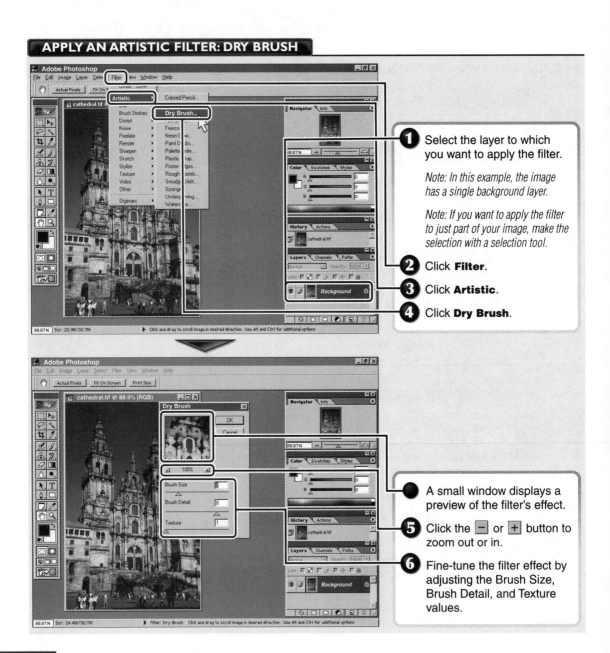

1 Select the layer to which you want to apply the filter.

Note: In this example, the image has a single background layer.

Note: If you want to apply the filter to just part of your image, make the selection with a selection tool.

2 Click **Filter**.

3 Click **Artistic**.

4 Click **Dry Brush**.

● A small window displays a preview of the filter's effect.

5 Click the ⊟ or ⊞ button to zoom out or in.

6 Fine-tune the filter effect by adjusting the Brush Size, Brush Detail, and Texture values.

in an instant

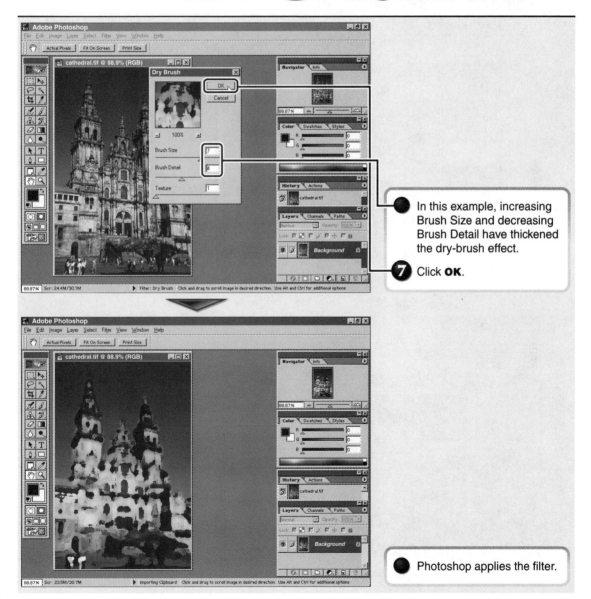

In this example, increasing Brush Size and decreasing Brush Detail have thickened the dry-brush effect.

7 Click **OK**.

Photoshop applies the filter.

APPLY A BLUR FILTER: GAUSSIAN BLUR

The Blur filters reduce the amount of detail in your image. The Gaussian Blur filter has advantages over the other Blur filters in that you can control the amount of blur added.

APPLY A BLUR FILTER: GAUSSIAN BLUR

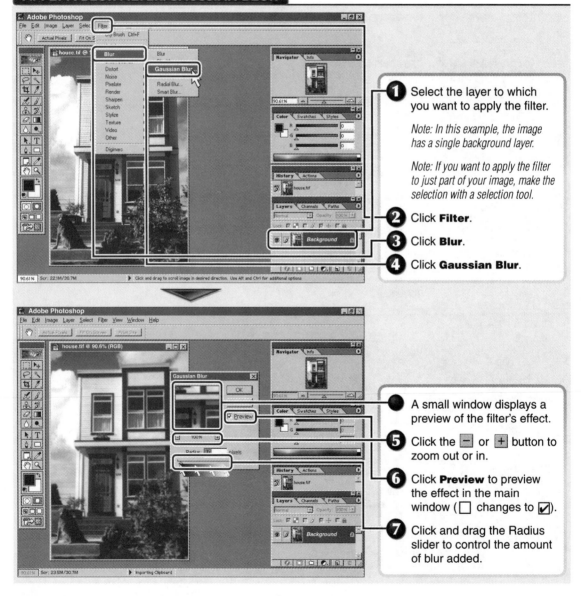

1 Select the layer to which you want to apply the filter.

Note: In this example, the image has a single background layer.

Note: If you want to apply the filter to just part of your image, make the selection with a selection tool.

2 Click **Filter**.

3 Click **Blur**.

4 Click **Gaussian Blur**.

A small window displays a preview of the filter's effect.

5 Click the ⊟ or ⊞ button to zoom out or in.

6 Click **Preview** to preview the effect in the main window (☐ changes to ☑).

7 Click and drag the Radius slider to control the amount of blur added.

in an *instant*

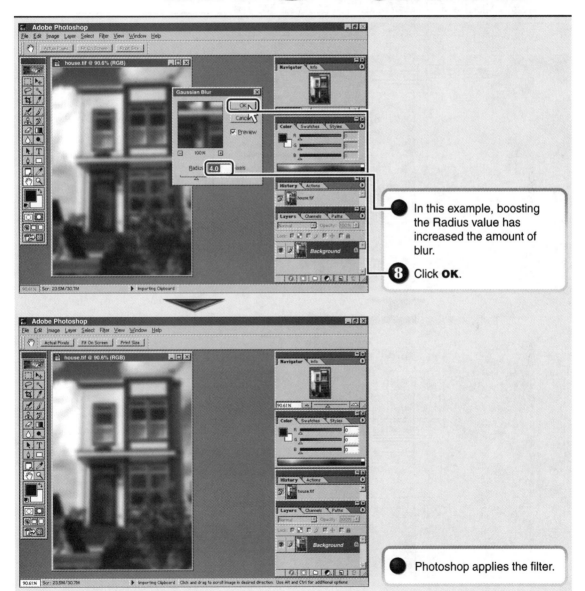

In this example, boosting the Radius value has increased the amount of blur.

8 Click **OK**.

Photoshop applies the filter.

The Brush Strokes filters make your image look painted. For example, the Crosshatch filter adds diagonal, overlapping brush-stroke effects to your image.

APPLY A BRUSH STROKES FILTER: CROSSHATCH

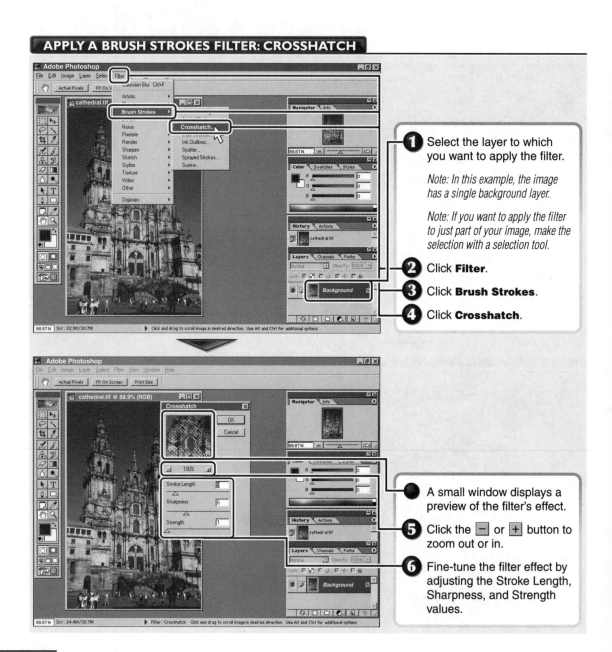

① Select the layer to which you want to apply the filter.

Note: In this example, the image has a single background layer.

Note: If you want to apply the filter to just part of your image, make the selection with a selection tool.

② Click **Filter**.

③ Click **Brush Strokes**.

④ Click **Crosshatch**.

■ A small window displays a preview of the filter's effect.

⑤ Click the ➖ or ➕ button to zoom out or in.

⑥ Fine-tune the filter effect by adjusting the Stroke Length, Sharpness, and Strength values.

in an *instant*

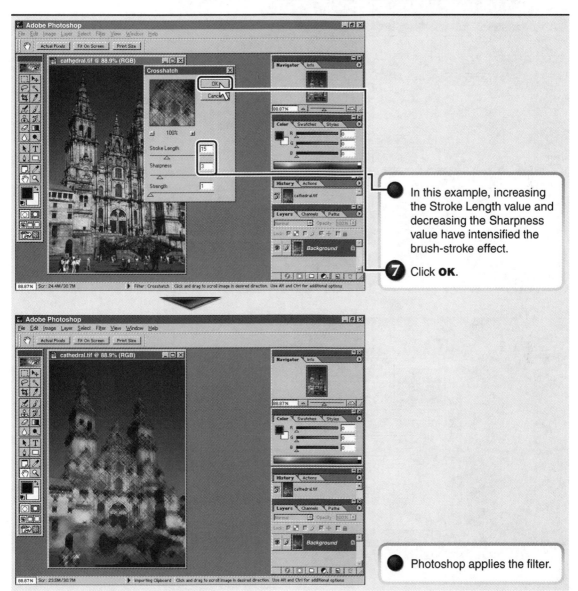

In this example, increasing the Stroke Length value and decreasing the Sharpness value have intensified the brush-stroke effect.

7 Click **OK**.

Photoshop applies the filter.

APPLY A DISTORT FILTER: SPHERIZE

The Distort filters stretch and squeeze areas of your image. For example, the Spherize filter makes your image look like it is being reflected off a mirrored sphere.

APPLY A DISTORT FILTER: SPHERIZE

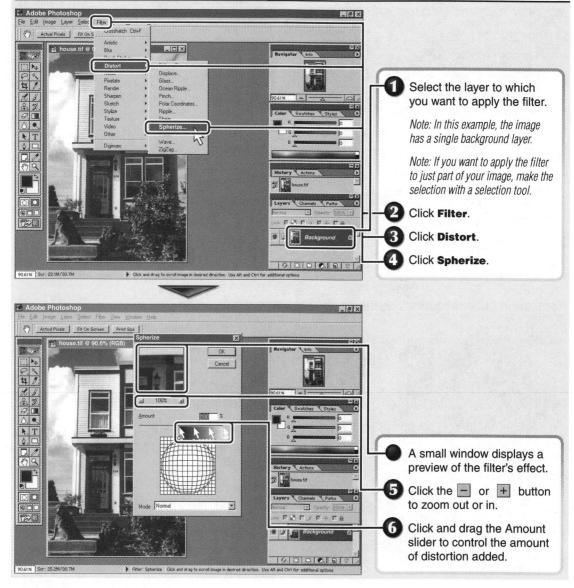

1 Select the layer to which you want to apply the filter.

Note: In this example, the image has a single background layer.

Note: If you want to apply the filter to just part of your image, make the selection with a selection tool.

2 Click **Filter**.

3 Click **Distort**.

4 Click **Spherize**.

■ A small window displays a preview of the filter's effect.

5 Click the ➖ or ➕ button to zoom out or in.

6 Click and drag the Amount slider to control the amount of distortion added.

166

in an *instant*

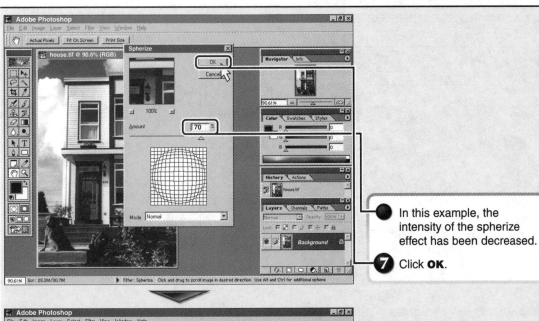

In this example, the
intensity of the spherize
effect has been decreased.

7 Click **OK**.

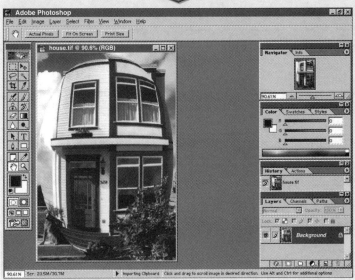

Photoshop applies the filter.

APPLY A NOISE FILTER: ADD NOISE

The Noise filters add or remove graininess in your image. You can add graininess to your image with the Add Noise filter.

APPLY A NOISE FILTER: ADD NOISE

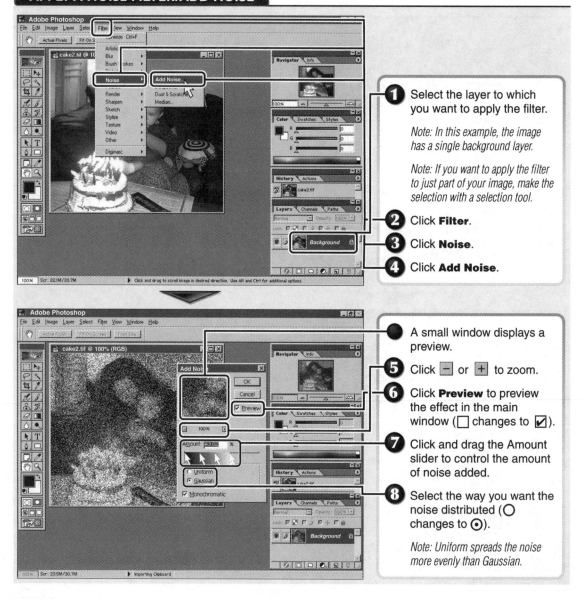

1 Select the layer to which you want to apply the filter.

Note: In this example, the image has a single background layer.

Note: If you want to apply the filter to just part of your image, make the selection with a selection tool.

2 Click **Filter**.

3 Click **Noise**.

4 Click **Add Noise**.

■ A small window displays a preview.

5 Click □ or ⊞ to zoom.

6 Click **Preview** to preview the effect in the main window (□ changes to ☑).

7 Click and drag the Amount slider to control the amount of noise added.

8 Select the way you want the noise distributed (○ changes to ⊙).

Note: Uniform spreads the noise more evenly than Gaussian.

in an *instant*

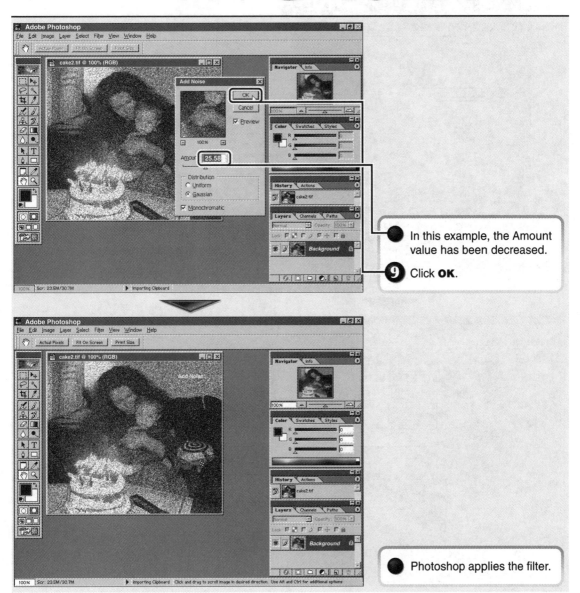

In this example, the Amount value has been decreased.

9 Click **OK**.

Photoshop applies the filter.

APPLY A PIXELATE FILTER: POINTILLIZE

The Pixelate filters divide areas of your image into solid-colored shapes. The Pointillize filter, for example, re-creates your image using colored dots.

APPLY A PIXELATE FILTER: POINTILLIZE

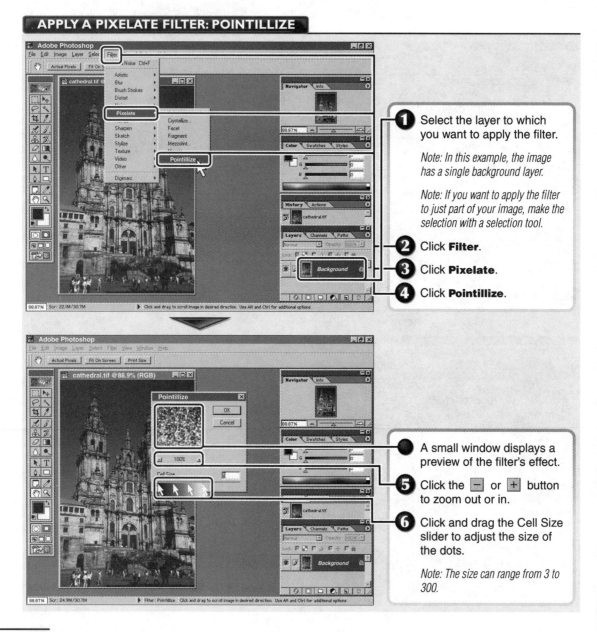

1 Select the layer to which you want to apply the filter.

Note: In this example, the image has a single background layer.

Note: If you want to apply the filter to just part of your image, make the selection with a selection tool.

2 Click **Filter**.

3 Click **Pixelate**.

4 Click **Pointillize**.

■ A small window displays a preview of the filter's effect.

5 Click the − or + button to zoom out or in.

6 Click and drag the Cell Size slider to adjust the size of the dots.

Note: The size can range from 3 to 300.

in an *instant*

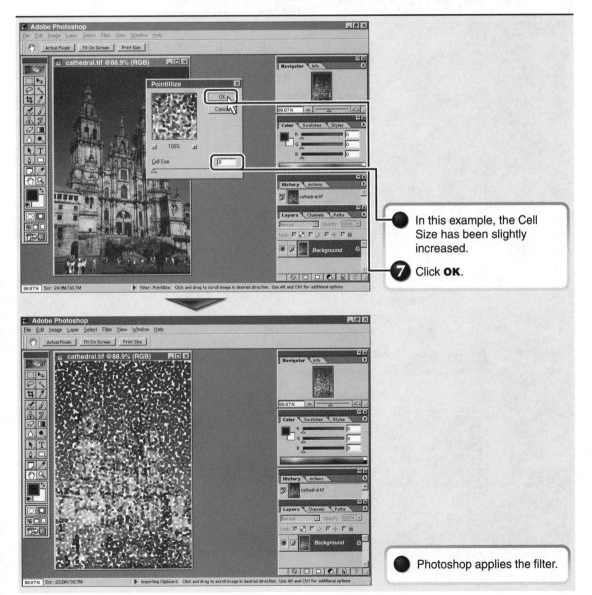

In this example, the Cell Size has been slightly increased.

7 Click **OK**.

Photoshop applies the filter.

APPLY A RENDER FILTER: LIGHTING EFFECTS

The Render filters use numeric techniques to apply effects to your image. The Lighting Effects filter, one example of a Render filter, lets you add spotlight and other lighting enhancements.

APPLY A RENDER FILTER: LIGHTING EFFECTS

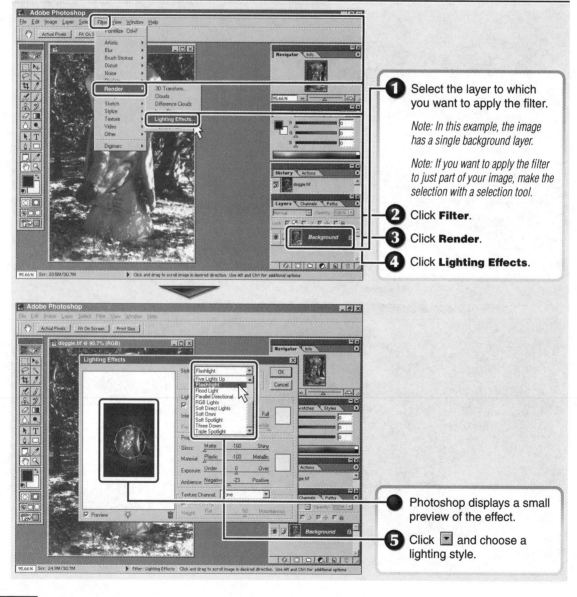

1 Select the layer to which you want to apply the filter.

Note: In this example, the image has a single background layer.

Note: If you want to apply the filter to just part of your image, make the selection with a selection tool.

2 Click **Filter**.

3 Click **Render**.

4 Click **Lighting Effects**.

● Photoshop displays a small preview of the effect.

5 Click ▾ and choose a lighting style.

172

in an *instant*

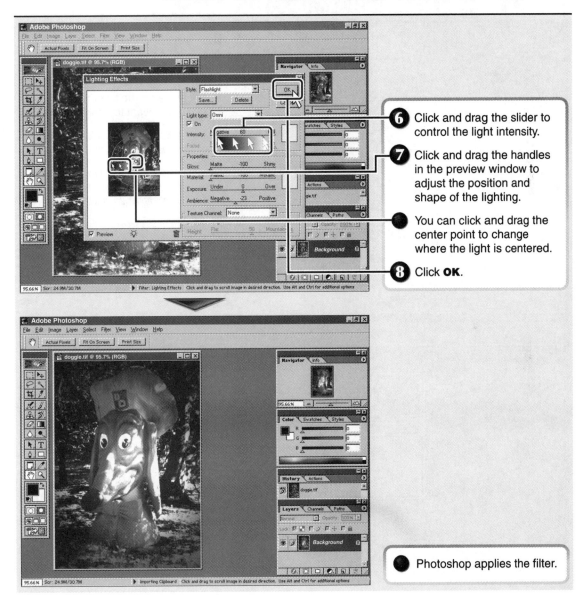

6 Click and drag the slider to control the light intensity.

7 Click and drag the handles in the preview window to adjust the position and shape of the lighting.

● You can click and drag the center point to change where the light is centered.

8 Click **OK**.

● Photoshop applies the filter.

APPLY A SHARPEN FILTER: UNSHARP MASK

The Sharpen filters intensify detail and reduce blurring in your image. The Unsharp Mask filter has an advantage over the other Sharpen filters in that it enables you to control the amount of sharpening applied.

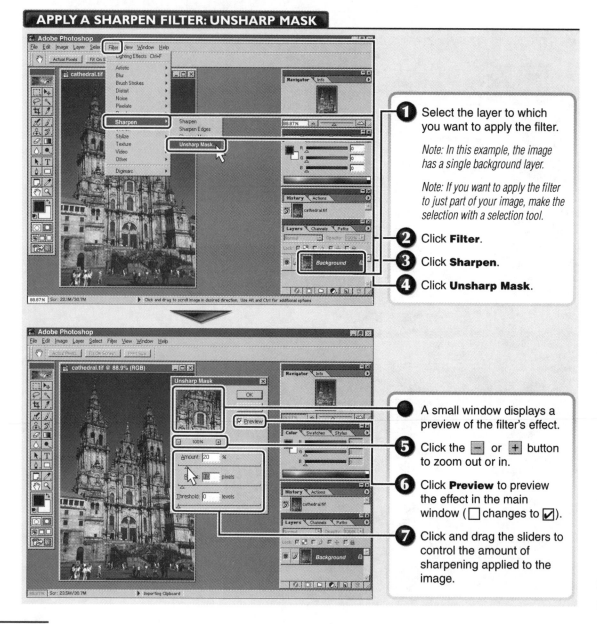

APPLY A SHARPEN FILTER: UNSHARP MASK

1 Select the layer to which you want to apply the filter.

Note: In this example, the image has a single background layer.

Note: If you want to apply the filter to just part of your image, make the selection with a selection tool.

2 Click **Filter**.

3 Click **Sharpen**.

4 Click **Unsharp Mask**.

■ A small window displays a preview of the filter's effect.

5 Click the ⊟ or ⊞ button to zoom out or in.

6 Click **Preview** to preview the effect in the main window (☐ changes to ☑).

7 Click and drag the sliders to control the amount of sharpening applied to the image.

in an *instant*

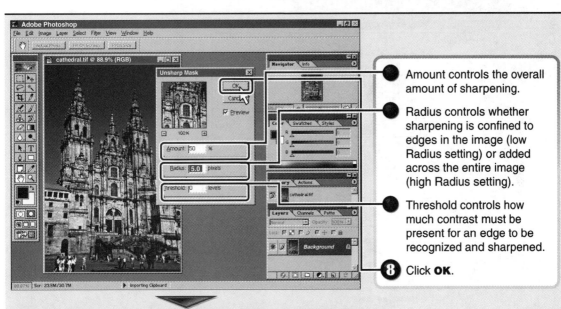

Amount controls the overall amount of sharpening.

Radius controls whether sharpening is confined to edges in the image (low Radius setting) or added across the entire image (high Radius setting).

Threshold controls how much contrast must be present for an edge to be recognized and sharpened.

8 Click **OK**.

Photoshop applies the filter.

APPLY A SKETCH FILTER: CHARCOAL

The Sketch filters add outlining effects to your image. The Charcoal filter, for example, makes an image look as if it was sketched by using charcoal on paper.

APPLY A SKETCH FILTER: CHARCOAL

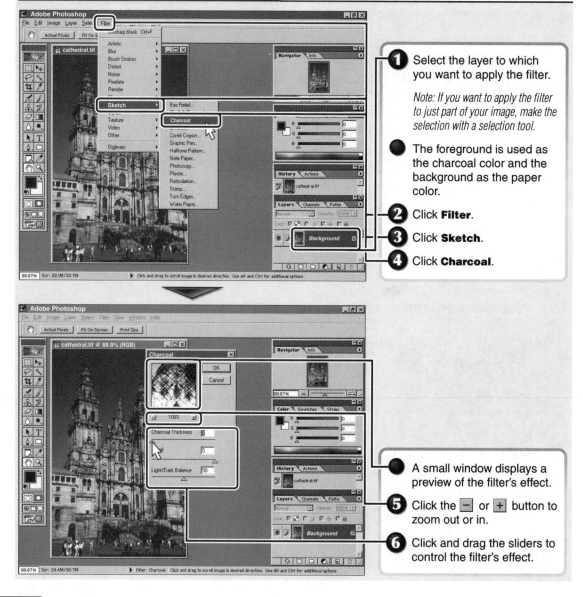

1 Select the layer to which you want to apply the filter.

Note: If you want to apply the filter to just part of your image, make the selection with a selection tool.

● The foreground is used as the charcoal color and the background as the paper color.

2 Click **Filter**.

3 Click **Sketch**.

4 Click **Charcoal**.

● A small window displays a preview of the filter's effect.

5 Click the ⊟ or ⊞ button to zoom out or in.

6 Click and drag the sliders to control the filter's effect.

176

in an *instant*

In this example, the thickness of the charcoal strokes has been increased. The Light/Dark Balance setting has also been increased to darken the image.

7 Click **OK**.

● Photoshop applies the filter.

APPLY A STYLIZE FILTER: GLOWING EDGES

The Stylize filters produce extreme artistic effects. For example, the Glowing Edges filter applies a neon effect to the edges in your image. Areas between the edges are turned black.

APPLY A STYLIZE FILTER: GLOWING EDGES

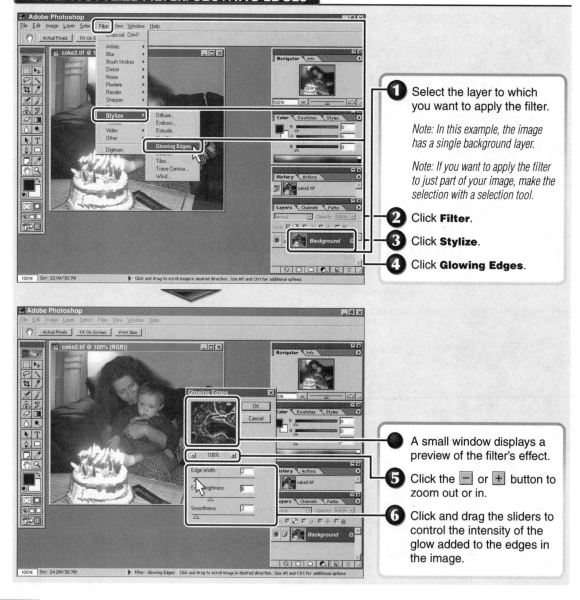

1 Select the layer to which you want to apply the filter.

Note: In this example, the image has a single background layer.

Note: If you want to apply the filter to just part of your image, make the selection with a selection tool.

2 Click **Filter**.

3 Click **Stylize**.

4 Click **Glowing Edges**.

■ A small window displays a preview of the filter's effect.

5 Click the ⊟ or ⊞ button to zoom out or in.

6 Click and drag the sliders to control the intensity of the glow added to the edges in the image.

in an *instant*

In this example, the Edge Width and Edge Brightness values have been increased to intensify the neon effect.

7 Click **OK**.

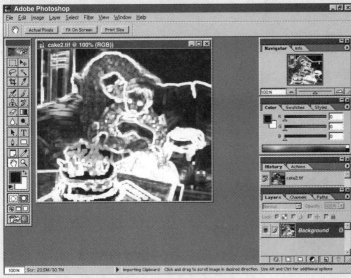

Photoshop applies the filter.

APPLY A TEXTURE FILTER: TEXTURIZER

The Texture filters let you apply patterns to your images. You can use the Texturizer filter to overlay different textures on your image.

APPLY A TEXTURE FILTER: TEXTURIZER

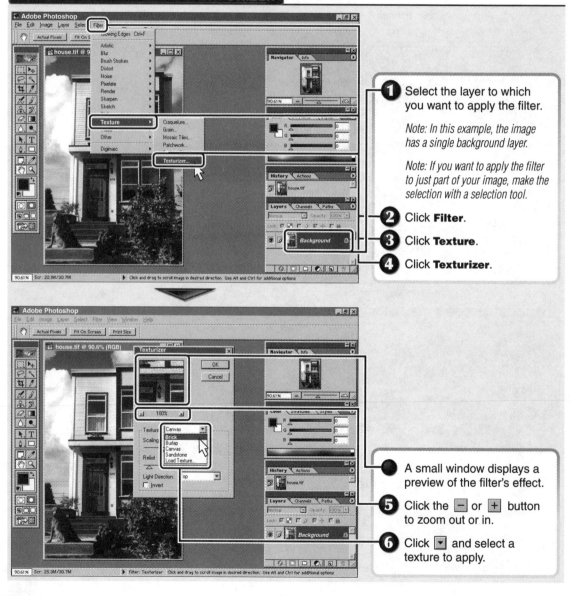

1 Select the layer to which you want to apply the filter.

Note: In this example, the image has a single background layer.

Note: If you want to apply the filter to just part of your image, make the selection with a selection tool.

2 Click **Filter**.

3 Click **Texture**.

4 Click **Texturizer**.

■ A small window displays a preview of the filter's effect.

5 Click the ⊟ or ⊞ button to zoom out or in.

6 Click ▾ and select a texture to apply.

in an instant

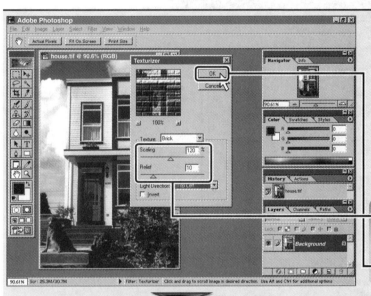

7 Adjust the sliders to control the intensity of the overlaid texture.

8 Click **OK**.

● Photoshop applies the filter.

APPLY A FILTER FROM THE OTHER SUBMENU: OFFSET

The filters in the Other submenu produce interesting effects that do not fall under the other menu descriptions. For example, the Offset filter lets you shift your image horizontally or vertically in the image window.

APPLY A FILTER FROM THE OTHER SUBMENU: OFFSET

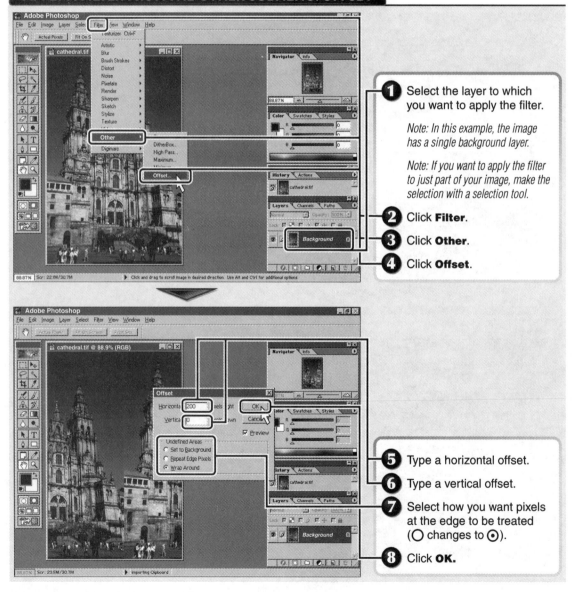

1 Select the layer to which you want to apply the filter.

Note: In this example, the image has a single background layer.

Note: If you want to apply the filter to just part of your image, make the selection with a selection tool.

2 Click **Filter**.

3 Click **Other**.

4 Click **Offset**.

5 Type a horizontal offset.

6 Type a vertical offset.

7 Select how you want pixels at the edge to be treated (O changes to ⊙).

8 Click **OK**.

in an *instant*

In this example, the image has been shifted horizontally (to the right) by adding a positive value to the Horizontal field.

Wrap Around was selected, so the pixels that leave the right edge of the image reappear on the left edge.

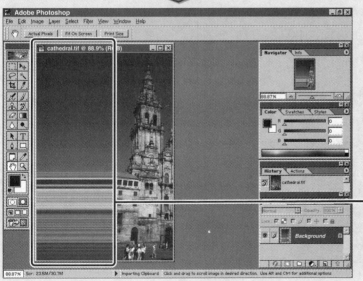

In this example, the same offset was applied but with Repeat Edge Pixels selected. This creates a streaked effect at the left edge.

ADD TYPE TO AN IMAGE

Adding type enables you to label elements in your images or use letters and words in artistic ways.

ADD TYPE TO AN IMAGE

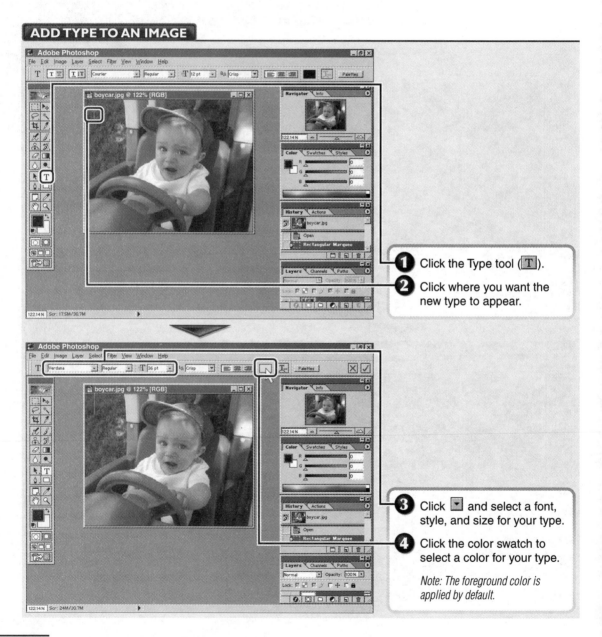

1 Click the Type tool (T).

2 Click where you want the new type to appear.

3 Click ☑ and select a font, style, and size for your type.

4 Click the color swatch to select a color for your type.

Note: The foreground color is applied by default.

in an *instant*

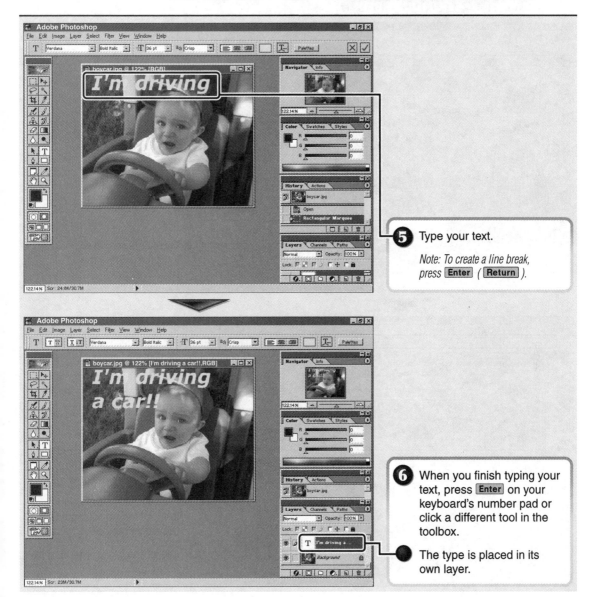

5 Type your text.

Note: To create a line break, press **Enter** *(* **Return** *).*

6 When you finish typing your text, press **Enter** on your keyboard's number pad or click a different tool in the toolbox.

■ The type is placed in its own layer.

ADD TYPE IN A BOUNDING BOX

You can add type inside a *bounding box* to constrain where the type appears and how it wraps.

ADD TYPE IN A BOUNDING BOX

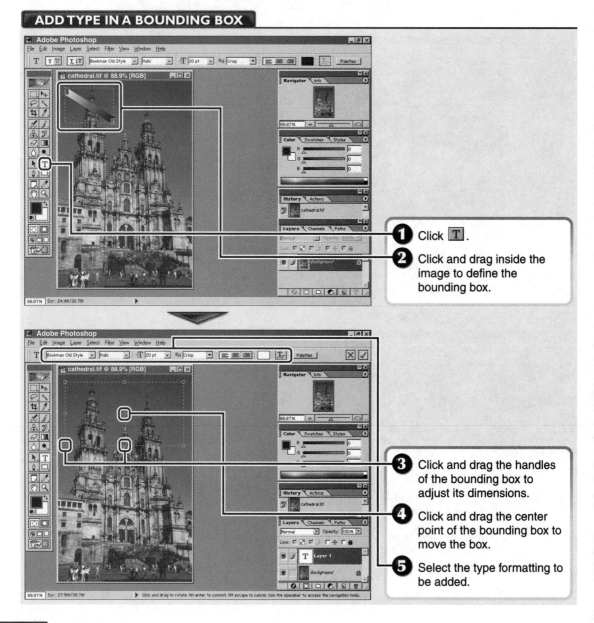

1 Click [T].

2 Click and drag inside the image to define the bounding box.

3 Click and drag the handles of the bounding box to adjust its dimensions.

4 Click and drag the center point of the bounding box to move the box.

5 Select the type formatting to be added.

in an *instant*

6 Type your text.

● Your text appears inside the bounding box with the formatting applied.

Note: When a line of text hits the edge of the bounding box, it automatically wraps to the next line.

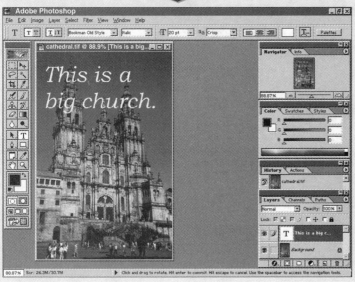

7 When you finish typing your text, press Enter on your keyboard's number pad or click a different tool in the toolbox.

● The bounding box disappears.

● To make the box reappear (in order to change its dimensions), click T and click the text.

CHANGE THE TYPE FORMATTING

You can change the font, style, size, and other characteristics of your type.

CHANGE THE TYPE FORMATTING

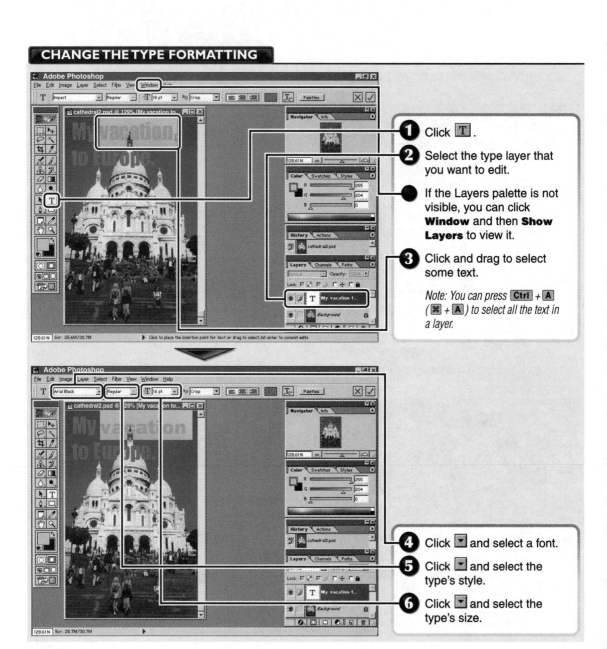

1 Click **T**.

2 Select the type layer that you want to edit.

● If the Layers palette is not visible, you can click **Window** and then **Show Layers** to view it.

3 Click and drag to select some text.

Note: You can press **Ctrl** + **A** *(* ⌘ + **A** *) to select all the text in a layer.*

4 Click ▼ and select a font.

5 Click ▼ and select the type's style.

6 Click ▼ and select the type's size.

in an *instant*

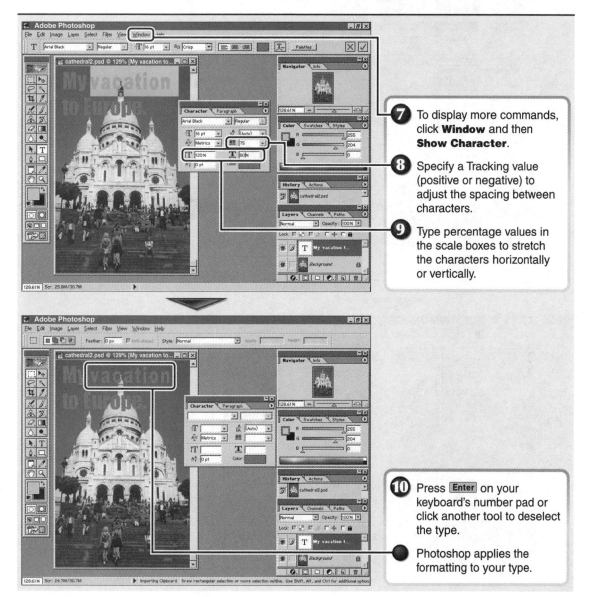

7 To display more commands, click **Window** and then **Show Character**.

8 Specify a Tracking value (positive or negative) to adjust the spacing between characters.

9 Type percentage values in the scale boxes to stretch the characters horizontally or vertically.

10 Press **Enter** on your keyboard's number pad or click another tool to deselect the type.

● Photoshop applies the formatting to your type.

CHANGE THE TYPE COLOR

You can change your type's color to make it blend or contrast with the rest of the image.

CHANGE THE TYPE COLOR

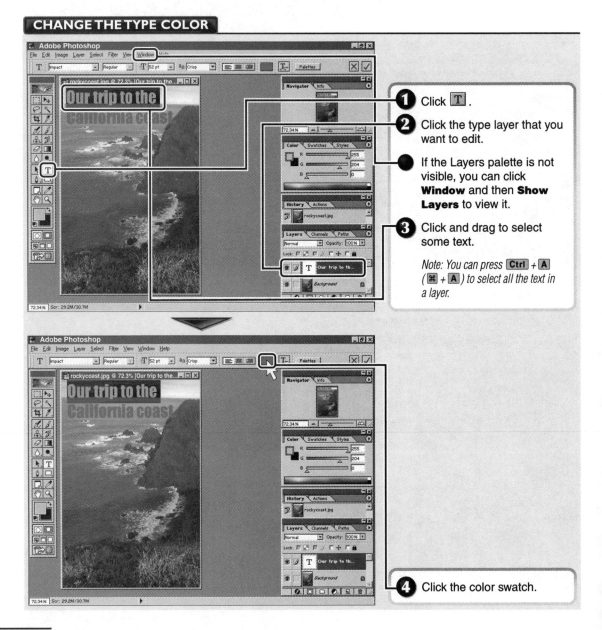

1 Click **T**.

2 Click the type layer that you want to edit.

■ If the Layers palette is not visible, you can click **Window** and then **Show Layers** to view it.

3 Click and drag to select some text.

Note: You can press **Ctrl** + **A** (⌘ + **A**) *to select all the text in a layer.*

4 Click the color swatch.

in an instant

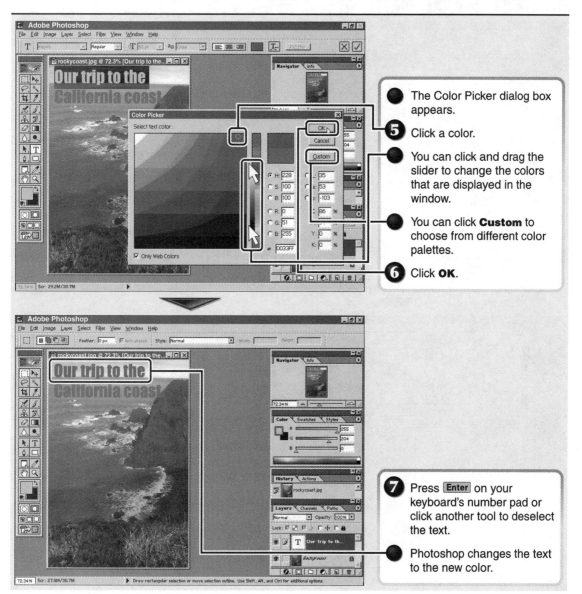

The Color Picker dialog box appears.

5 Click a color.

You can click and drag the slider to change the colors that are displayed in the window.

You can click **Custom** to choose from different color palettes.

6 Click **OK**.

7 Press **Enter** on your keyboard's number pad or click another tool to deselect the text.

Photoshop changes the text to the new color.

APPLY A FILTER TO TYPE

To apply a filter to type, you must first rasterize the type. Rasterizing converts your type layer into a regular Photoshop layer. Rasterized type can no longer be edited using the type tools.

APPLY A FILTER TO TYPE

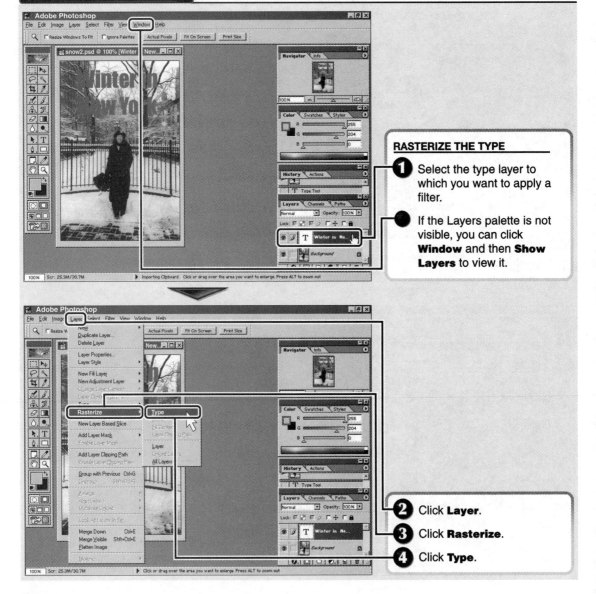

RASTERIZE THE TYPE

1 Select the type layer to which you want to apply a filter.

If the Layers palette is not visible, you can click **Window** and then **Show Layers** to view it.

2 Click **Layer**.

3 Click **Rasterize**.

4 Click **Type**.

in an *instant*

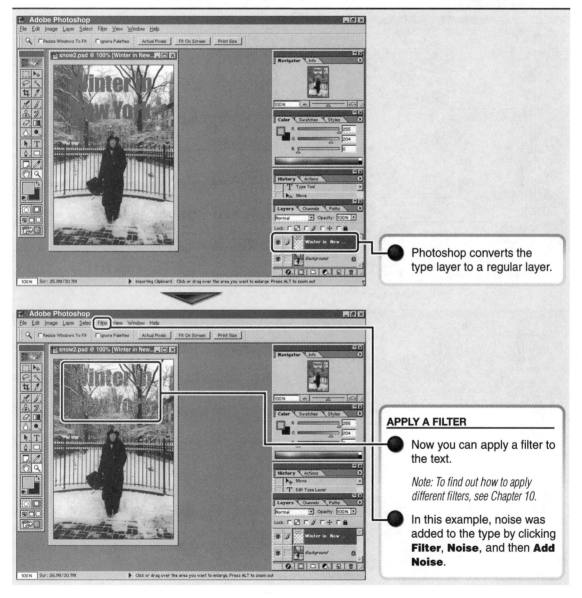

Photoshop converts the
type layer to a regular layer.

APPLY A FILTER

Now you can apply a filter to
the text.

*Note: To find out how to apply
different filters, see Chapter 10.*

In this example, noise was
added to the type by clicking
Filter, **Noise**, and then **Add
Noise**.

Photoshop's Warp feature lets you easily bend and distort layers of type.

WARP TYPE

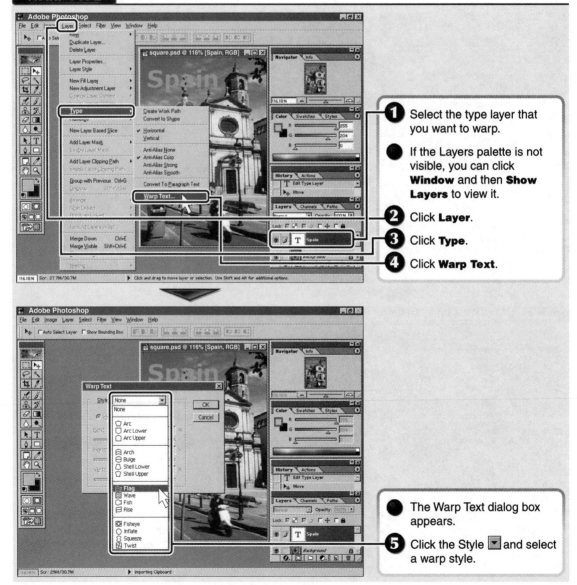

① Select the type layer that you want to warp.

● If the Layers palette is not visible, you can click **Window** and then **Show Layers** to view it.

② Click **Layer**.

③ Click **Type**.

④ Click **Warp Text**.

● The Warp Text dialog box appears.

⑤ Click the Style ▼ and select a warp style.

in an *instant*

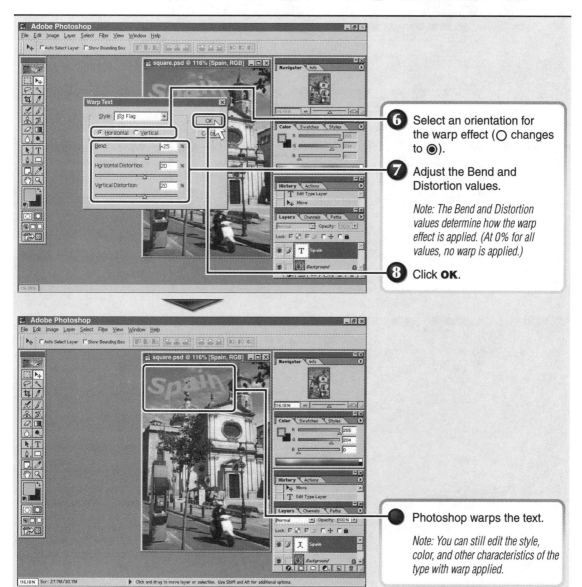

6 Select an orientation for the warp effect (○ changes to ◉).

7 Adjust the Bend and Distortion values.

Note: The Bend and Distortion values determine how the warp effect is applied. (At 0% for all values, no warp is applied.)

8 Click **OK**.

● Photoshop warps the text.

Note: You can still edit the style, color, and other characteristics of the type with warp applied.

RECORD AN ACTION

You can record a sequence of commands as an action and replay it on other image files. This saves time when you have a Photoshop task that you need to repeat.

RECORD AN ACTION

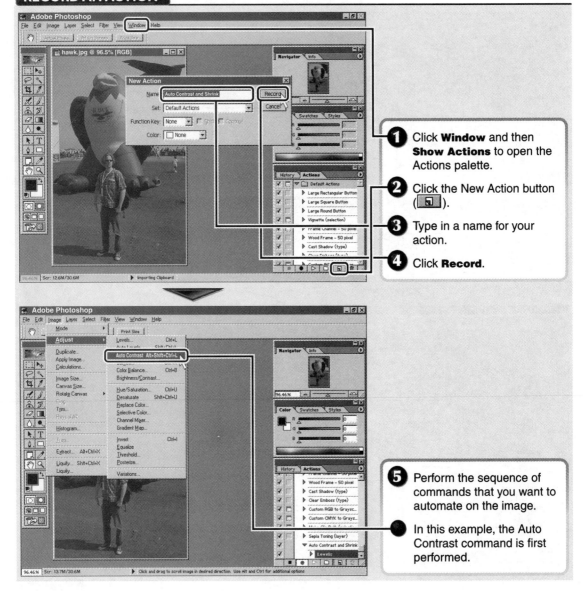

1 Click **Window** and then **Show Actions** to open the Actions palette.

2 Click the New Action button (▣).

3 Type in a name for your action.

4 Click **Record**.

5 Perform the sequence of commands that you want to automate on the image.

● In this example, the Auto Contrast command is first performed.

in an *instant*

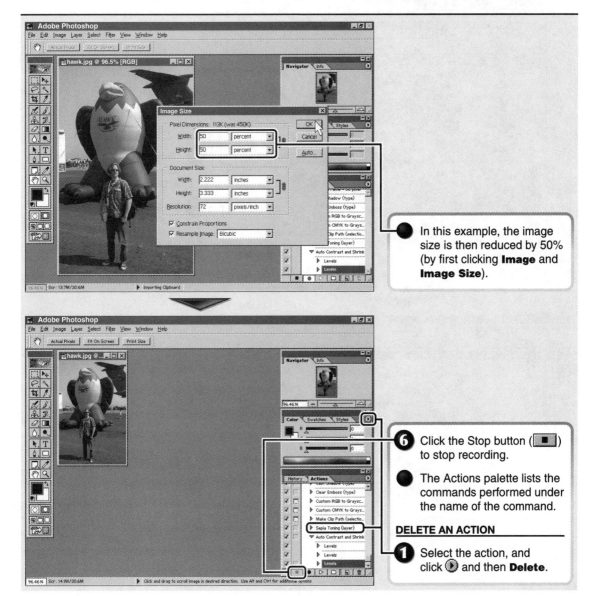

In this example, the image size is then reduced by 50% (by first clicking **Image** and **Image Size**).

6 Click the Stop button (▪) to stop recording.

The Actions palette lists the commands performed under the name of the command.

DELETE AN ACTION

1 Select the action, and click 🔘 and then **Delete**.

197

PLAY AN ACTION

You can play an action from the Actions palette on an image. This saves time by letting you execute multiple Photoshop commands with a single click.

PLAY A SINGLE ACTION

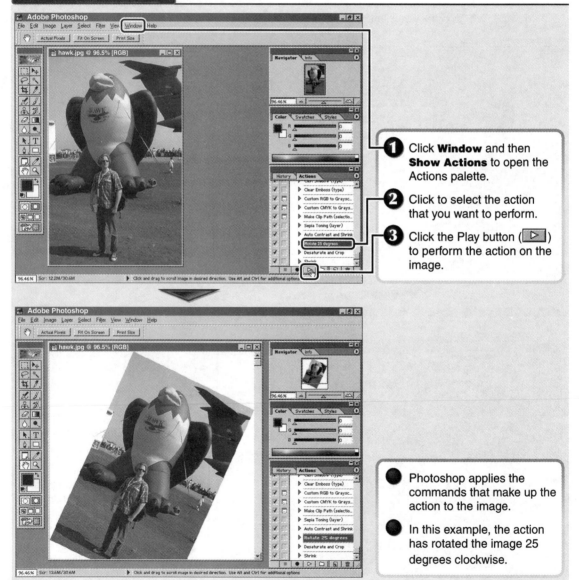

① Click **Window** and then **Show Actions** to open the Actions palette.

② Click to select the action that you want to perform.

③ Click the Play button (▷) to perform the action on the image.

● Photoshop applies the commands that make up the action to the image.

● In this example, the action has rotated the image 25 degrees clockwise.

in an instant

PLAY MULTIPLE ACTIONS

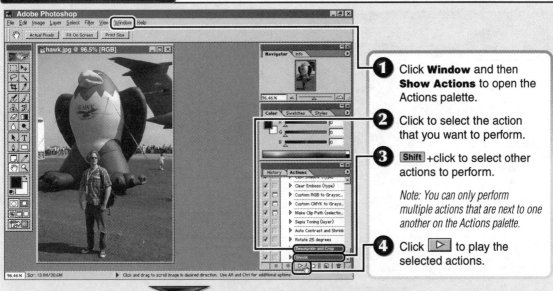

1. Click **Window** and then **Show Actions** to open the Actions palette.

2. Click to select the action that you want to perform.

3. Shift +click to select other actions to perform.

   Note: You can only perform multiple actions that are next to one another on the Actions palette.

4. Click ▷ to play the selected actions.

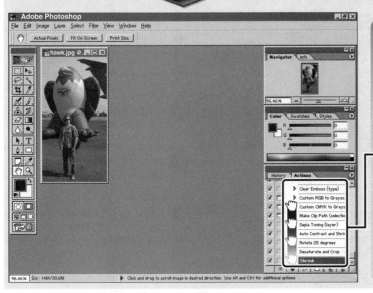

● Photoshop performs the actions in the order they are listed in the Actions palette.

● In this example, the image is desaturated and cropped and then has its size reduced.

● To rearrange the order of actions in the Actions palette, you can click and drag them up and down.

   Note: Not all actions can be played on all images. For example, you cannot play a Color Balance action on a grayscale image.

CREATE AND APPLY A DROPLET

You can store an action as an icon in a folder on your computer. You can then drag and drop image files or folders of image files onto this icon, called a *droplet*, to apply the action.

CREATE A DROPLET

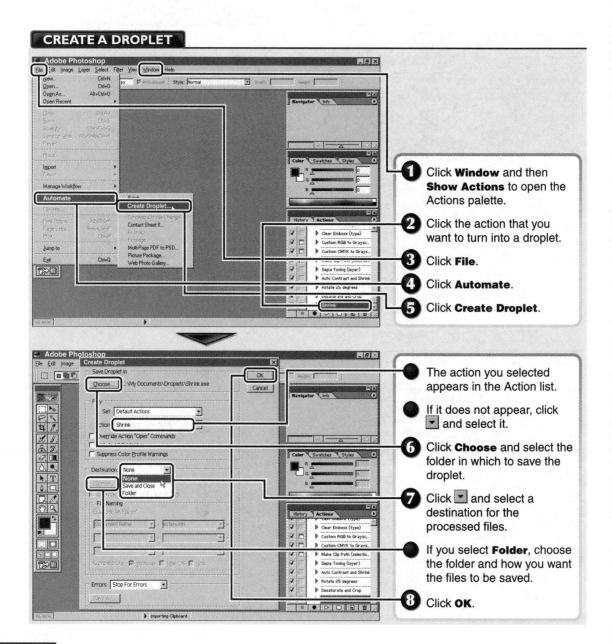

1 Click **Window** and then **Show Actions** to open the Actions palette.

2 Click the action that you want to turn into a droplet.

3 Click **File**.

4 Click **Automate**.

5 Click **Create Droplet**.

■ The action you selected appears in the Action list.

■ If it does not appear, click ▾ and select it.

6 Click **Choose** and select the folder in which to save the droplet.

7 Click ▾ and select a destination for the processed files.

■ If you select **Folder**, choose the folder and how you want the files to be saved.

8 Click **OK**.

in an *instant*

APPLY A DROPLET

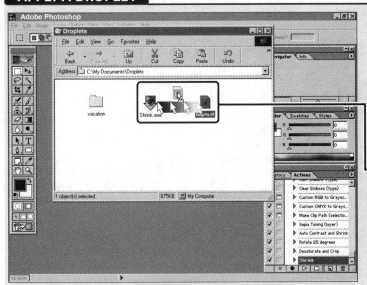

1 Navigate to the folder where you saved the droplet in the file directory system of your computer.

2 Click and drag an image file onto the droplet icon.

Note: You do not need to have Photoshop open to apply a droplet. Photoshop automatically opens after you drop your file onto the droplet.

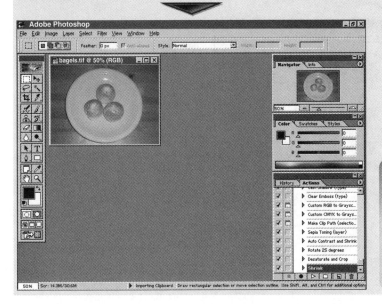

● Photoshop applies the droplet's action to the image.

Note: There is no Undo command for droplet actions. It is a good idea to use copies of your original files when applying droplets in case you change your mind.

CREATE A VIGNETTE EFFECT

You can create a soft edge in your image by using the Vignette action. Vignette is one of the actions that comes prebuilt in Photoshop's Actions palette.

CREATE A VIGNETTE EFFECT

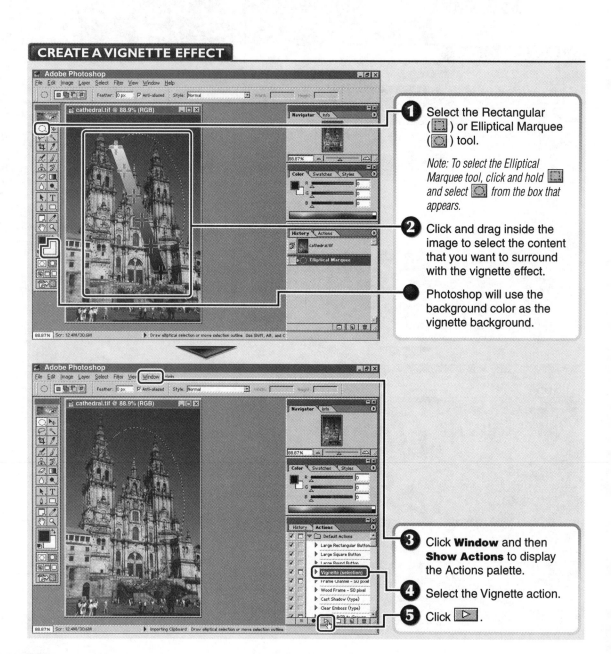

1 Select the Rectangular (▢) or Elliptical Marquee (◯) tool.

Note: To select the Elliptical Marquee tool, click and hold ▢ and select ◯ from the box that appears.

2 Click and drag inside the image to select the content that you want to surround with the vignette effect.

■ Photoshop will use the background color as the vignette background.

3 Click **Window** and then **Show Actions** to display the Actions palette.

4 Select the Vignette action.

5 Click ▷.

in an *instant*

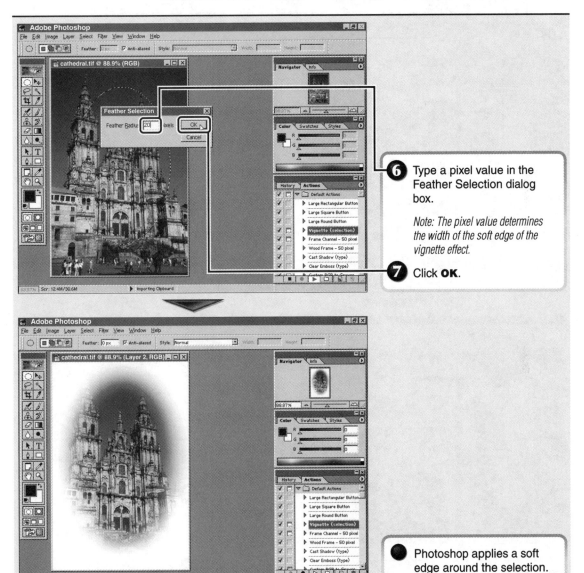

6 Type a pixel value in the Feather Selection dialog box.

Note: The pixel value determines the width of the soft edge of the vignette effect.

7 Click **OK**.

● Photoshop applies a soft edge around the selection.

CREATE BUTTONS

Photoshop comes with several prebuilt actions that automatically create small buttons on your image.

CREATE BUTTONS

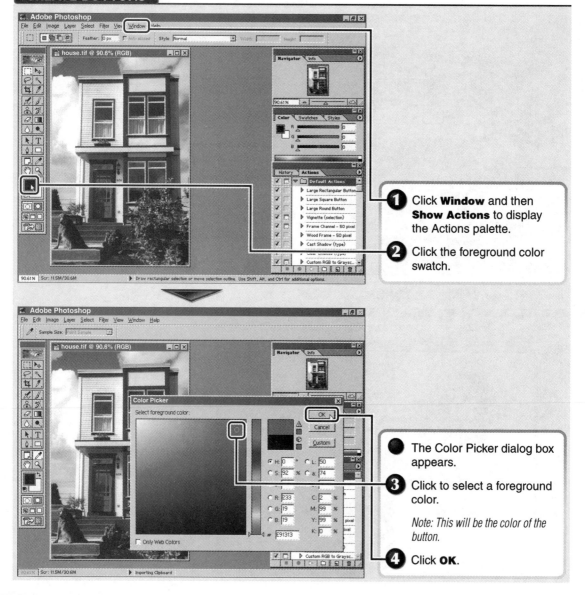

1 Click **Window** and then **Show Actions** to display the Actions palette.

2 Click the foreground color swatch.

● The Color Picker dialog box appears.

3 Click to select a foreground color.

Note: This will be the color of the button.

4 Click **OK**.

in an *instant*

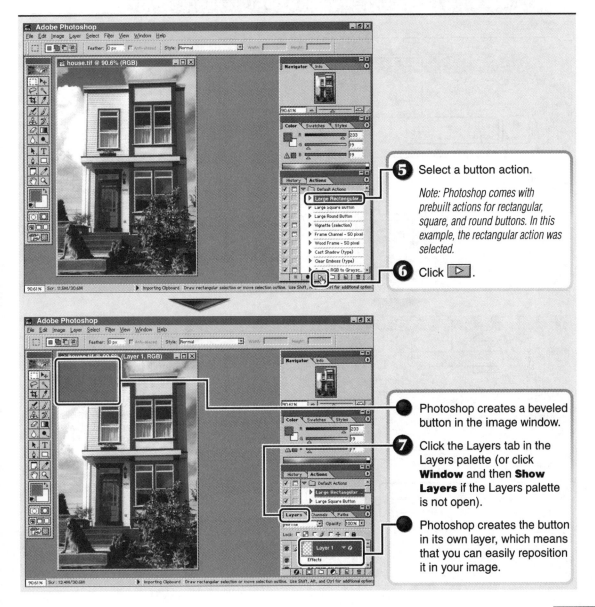

5 Select a button action.

Note: Photoshop comes with prebuilt actions for rectangular, square, and round buttons. In this example, the rectangular action was selected.

6 Click ▷ .

■ Photoshop creates a beveled button in the image window.

7 Click the Layers tab in the Layers palette (or click **Window** and then **Show Layers** if the Layers palette is not open).

■ Photoshop creates the button in its own layer, which means that you can easily reposition it in your image.

APPLY AN ACTION TO MULTIPLE IMAGES BY BATCH PROCESSING

You can automatically apply an action to multiple images with the Batch command. The Batch command is a great time-saver for repetitive tasks such as optimizing large numbers of digital photos.

APPLY AN ACTION TO MULTIPLE IMAGES BY BATCH PROCESSING

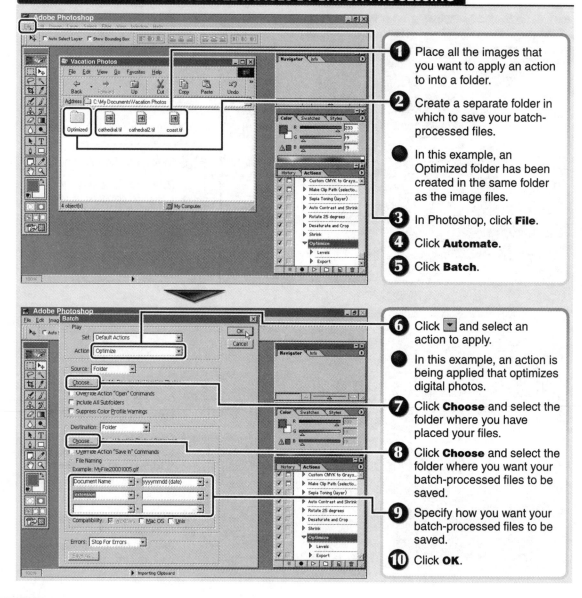

1 Place all the images that you want to apply an action to into a folder.

2 Create a separate folder in which to save your batch-processed files.

● In this example, an Optimized folder has been created in the same folder as the image files.

3 In Photoshop, click **File**.

4 Click **Automate**.

5 Click **Batch**.

6 Click ▼ and select an action to apply.

● In this example, an action is being applied that optimizes digital photos.

7 Click **Choose** and select the folder where you have placed your files.

8 Click **Choose** and select the folder where you want your batch-processed files to be saved.

9 Specify how you want your batch-processed files to be saved.

10 Click **OK**.

in an instant

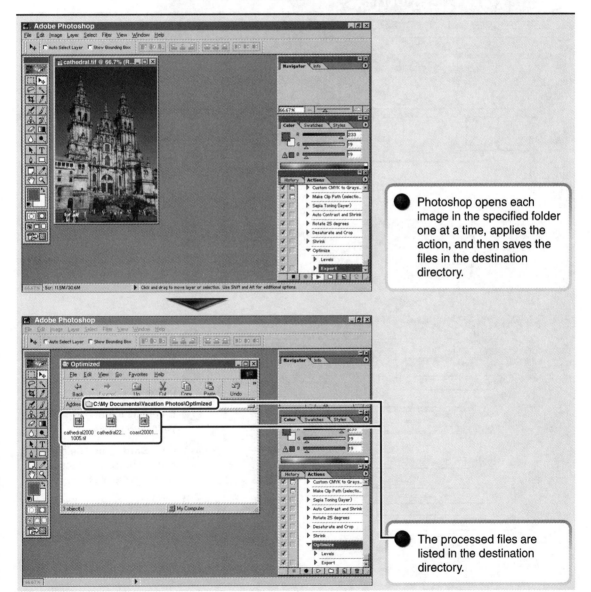

Photoshop opens each image in the specified folder one at a time, applies the action, and then saves the files in the destination directory.

The processed files are listed in the destination directory.

CREATE A WEB PHOTO GALLERY

You can automatically create a Web site photo gallery that showcases your images. Photoshop not only sizes and optimizes your image files, but it also creates the Web pages that display the images and links those pages together.

CREATE A WEB PHOTO GALLERY

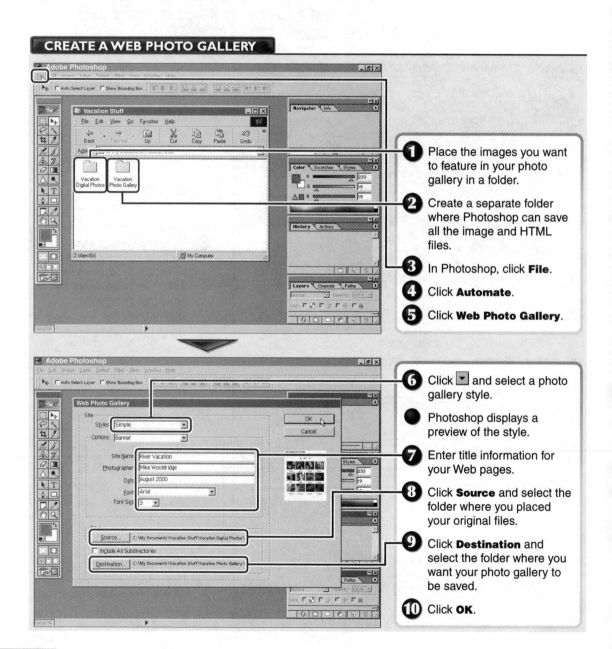

1 Place the images you want to feature in your photo gallery in a folder.

2 Create a separate folder where Photoshop can save all the image and HTML files.

3 In Photoshop, click **File**.

4 Click **Automate**.

5 Click **Web Photo Gallery**.

6 Click ⏷ and select a photo gallery style.

■ Photoshop displays a preview of the style.

7 Enter title information for your Web pages.

8 Click **Source** and select the folder where you placed your original files.

9 Click **Destination** and select the folder where you want your photo gallery to be saved.

10 Click **OK**.

208

in an instant

Photoshop opens each image in the specified folder, creates versions for the photo gallery, and generates the necessary HTML code.

After the processing is complete, Photoshop opens the default Web browser on your computer and displays the home page of the gallery.

11 Click a thumbnail to see a larger version of the image.

SAVE A PHOTOSHOP IMAGE

You can save an image in Photoshop's native image format. This format enables you to retain multiple image layers.

SAVE A PHOTOSHOP IMAGE

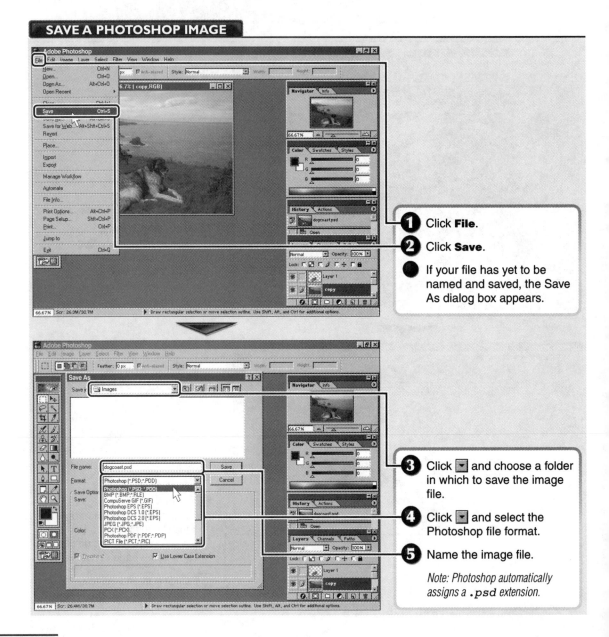

① Click **File**.

② Click **Save**.

● If your file has yet to be named and saved, the Save As dialog box appears.

③ Click ▼ and choose a folder in which to save the image file.

④ Click ▼ and select the Photoshop file format.

⑤ Name the image file.

Note: Photoshop automatically assigns a .psd extension.

in an *instant*

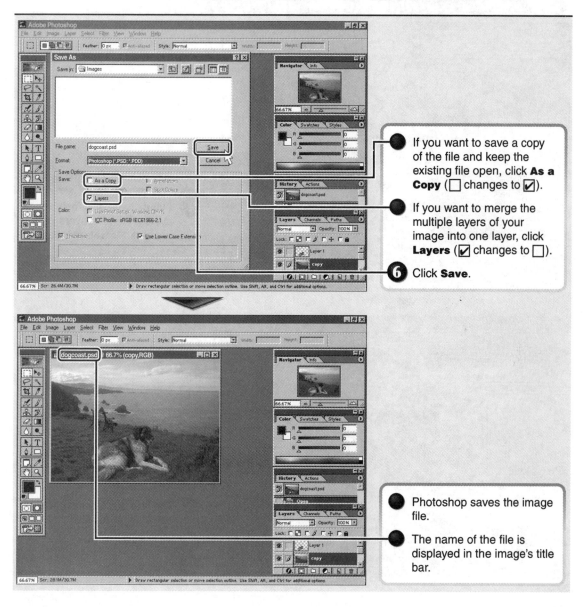

If you want to save a copy of the file and keep the existing file open, click **As a Copy** (☐ changes to ☑).

If you want to merge the multiple layers of your image into one layer, click **Layers** (☑ changes to ☐).

6 Click **Save**.

Photoshop saves the image file.

The name of the file is displayed in the image's title bar.

SAVE AN IMAGE FOR USE IN ANOTHER APPLICATION

You can save your image in a format that can be used in other imaging or page-layout applications. TIFF (Tagged Image File Format) and EPS (Encapsulated PostScript) are standard formats that are supported by many applications on both Windows and Macintosh platforms.

SAVE AN IMAGE FOR USE IN ANOTHER APPLICATION

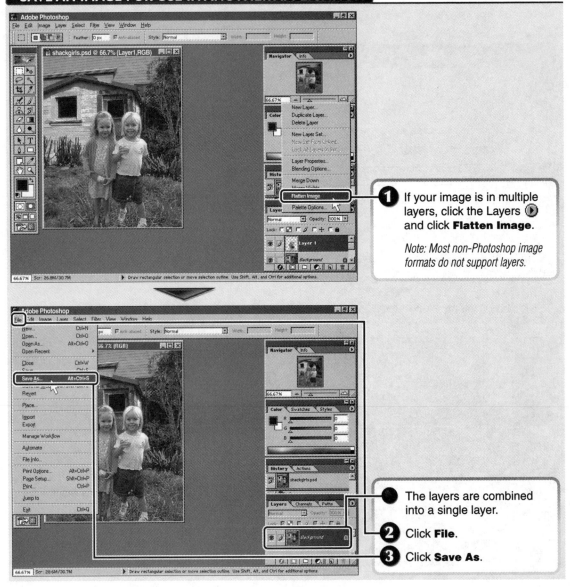

1 If your image is in multiple layers, click the Layers (▶) and click **Flatten Image**.

Note: Most non-Photoshop image formats do not support layers.

The layers are combined into a single layer.

2 Click **File**.

3 Click **Save As**.

in an instant

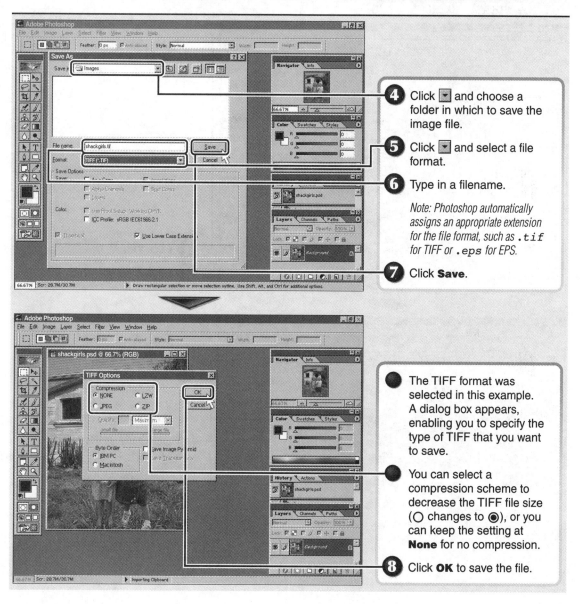

④ Click ▾ and choose a folder in which to save the image file.

⑤ Click ▾ and select a file format.

⑥ Type in a filename.

Note: Photoshop automatically assigns an appropriate extension for the file format, such as .tif for TIFF or .eps for EPS.

⑦ Click **Save**.

● The TIFF format was selected in this example. A dialog box appears, enabling you to specify the type of TIFF that you want to save.

● You can select a compression scheme to decrease the TIFF file size (○ changes to ◉), or you can keep the setting at **None** for no compression.

⑧ Click **OK** to save the file.

213

SAVE A JPEG FOR THE WEB

You can save a Photoshop image in the JPEG (Joint Photographic Experts Group) format and publish it on the Web. JPEG is the preferred file format for saving photographic images for the Web.

SAVE A JPEG FOR THE WEB

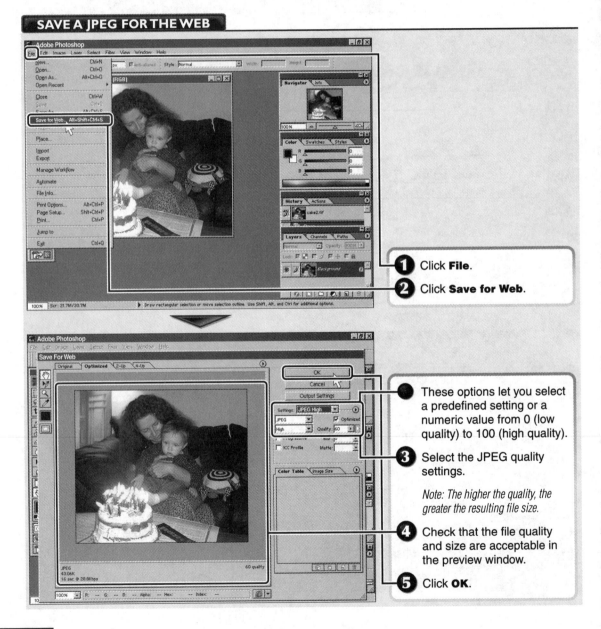

1 Click **File**.

2 Click **Save for Web**.

● These options let you select a predefined setting or a numeric value from 0 (low quality) to 100 (high quality).

3 Select the JPEG quality settings.

Note: The higher the quality, the greater the resulting file size.

4 Check that the file quality and size are acceptable in the preview window.

5 Click **OK**.

in an *instant*

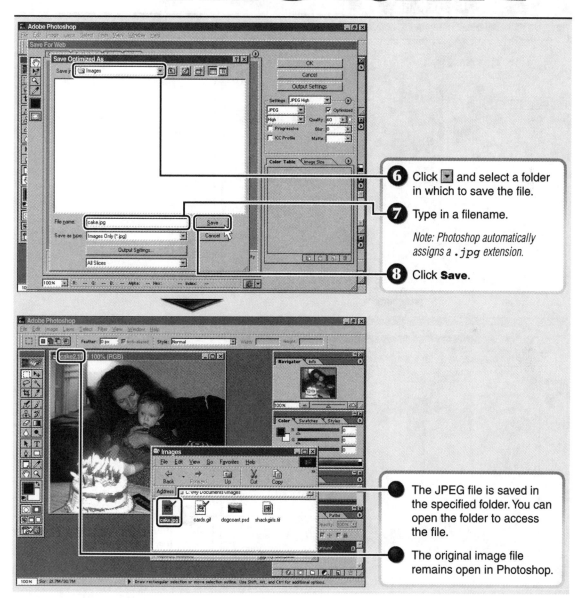

6 Click ▼ and select a folder in which to save the file.

7 Type in a filename.

Note: Photoshop automatically assigns a .jpg extension.

8 Click **Save**.

■ The JPEG file is saved in the specified folder. You can open the folder to access the file.

■ The original image file remains open in Photoshop.

SAVE A GIF FOR THE WEB

You can save a file as a GIF (Graphics Interchange Format) and publish it on the Web. GIF image files are good for illustrations that have a lot of solid color.

SAVE A GIF FOR THE WEB

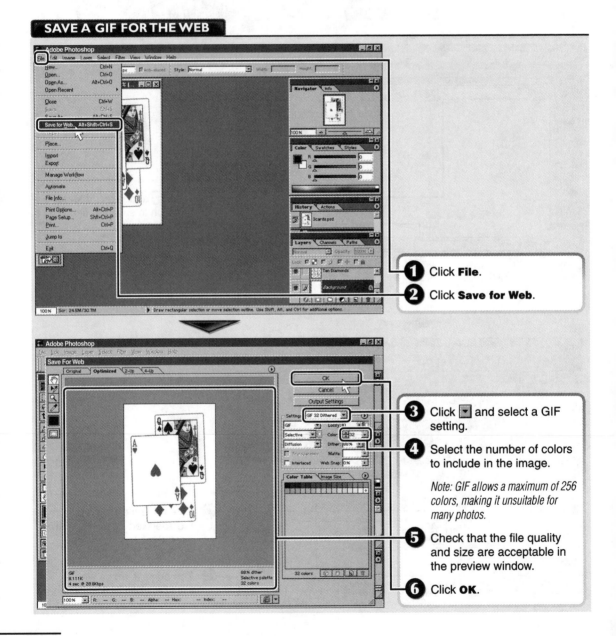

1 Click **File**.

2 Click **Save for Web**.

3 Click ▼ and select a GIF setting.

4 Select the number of colors to include in the image.

Note: GIF allows a maximum of 256 colors, making it unsuitable for many photos.

5 Check that the file quality and size are acceptable in the preview window.

6 Click **OK**.

in an *instant*

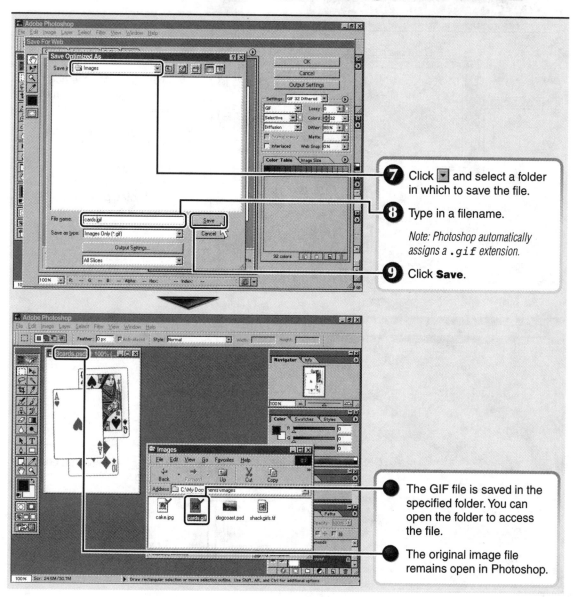

7 Click ▼ and select a folder in which to save the file.

8 Type in a filename.

Note: Photoshop automatically assigns a .gif extension.

9 Click **Save**.

● The GIF file is saved in the specified folder. You can open the folder to access the file.

● The original image file remains open in Photoshop.

SAVE A GIF WITH TRANSPARENCY

You can include transparent pixels in GIF files. The transparent pixels do not show up on Web pages, which is ideal for floating images or icons. You need to work with non-Background layers to create transparent GIFs because Background layers cannot contain transparent pixels.

SAVE A GIF WITH TRANSPARENCY

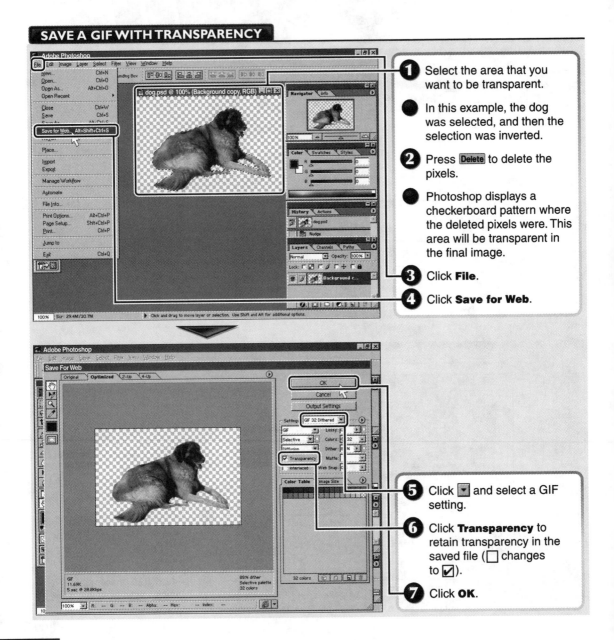

① Select the area that you want to be transparent.

● In this example, the dog was selected, and then the selection was inverted.

② Press Delete to delete the pixels.

● Photoshop displays a checkerboard pattern where the deleted pixels were. This area will be transparent in the final image.

③ Click **File**.

④ Click **Save for Web**.

⑤ Click ▼ and select a GIF setting.

⑥ Click **Transparency** to retain transparency in the saved file (☐ changes to ☑).

⑦ Click **OK**.

in an *instant*

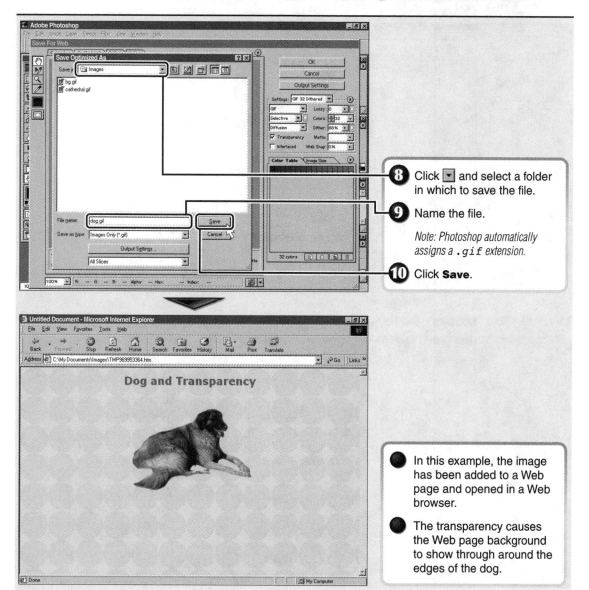

8 Click ▼ and select a folder in which to save the file.

9 Name the file.

Note: Photoshop automatically assigns a .gif extension.

10 Click **Save**.

● In this example, the image has been added to a Web page and opened in a Web browser.

● The transparency causes the Web page background to show through around the edges of the dog.

SAVE A GIF WITH WEB-SAFE COLORS

You can save your GIF images using Web-safe colors.
This ensures that the images appear the way you
expect in browsers running on 256-color monitors.

SAVE A GIF WITH WEB-SAFE COLORS

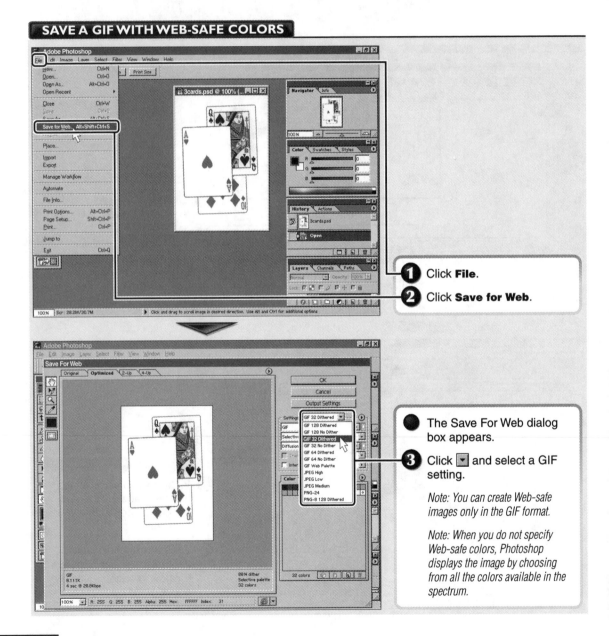

1 Click **File**.

2 Click **Save for Web**.

■ The Save For Web dialog box appears.

3 Click ▼ and select a GIF setting.

Note: You can create Web-safe images only in the GIF format.

Note: When you do not specify Web-safe colors, Photoshop displays the image by choosing from all the colors available in the spectrum.

in an *instant*

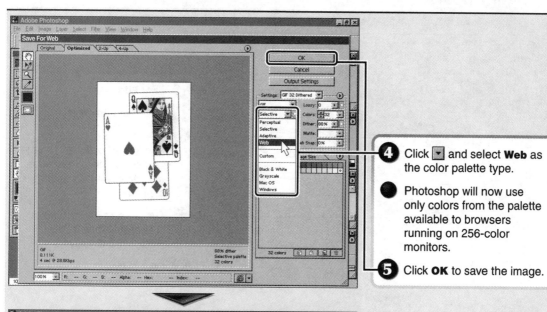

4 Click and select **Web** as the color palette type.

● Photoshop will now use only colors from the palette available to browsers running on 256-color monitors.

5 Click **OK** to save the image.

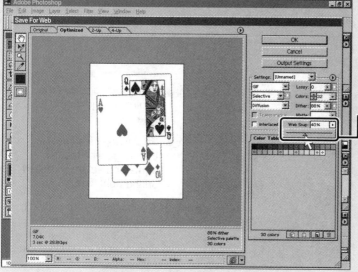

MAKE A GIF PARTIALLY WEB-SAFE

● You can specify a degree of Web safety (from 1% to 100%) in your image by using the Web Snap slider.

Note: The Web Snap slider lets you compromise between creating a totally Web-safe image (which may display poorly) and creating an image that has no Web-safe colors at all.

COMPARE FILE SIZES

You can compare the results of different compression schemes on your Web images. This helps you choose which scheme is most efficient and generates the best-looking image. You can then save the image using that scheme.

COMPARE FILE SIZES

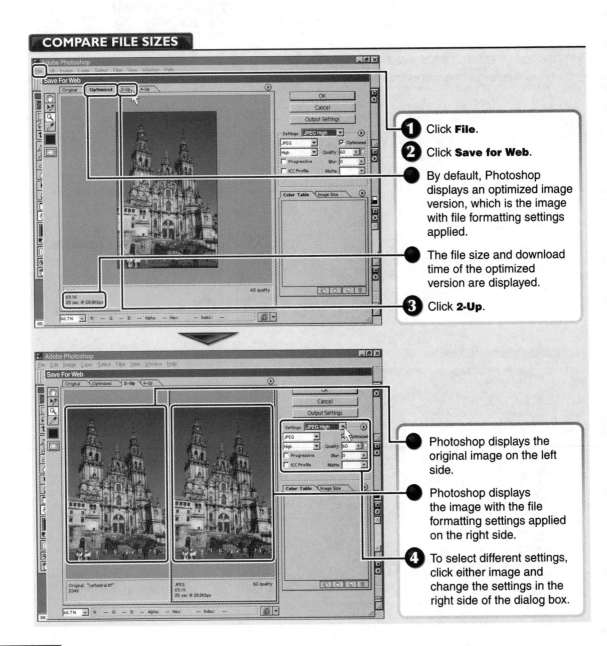

1 Click **File**.

2 Click **Save for Web**.

By default, Photoshop displays an optimized image version, which is the image with file formatting settings applied.

The file size and download time of the optimized version are displayed.

3 Click **2-Up**.

Photoshop displays the original image on the left side.

Photoshop displays the image with the file formatting settings applied on the right side.

4 To select different settings, click either image and change the settings in the right side of the dialog box.

in an instant

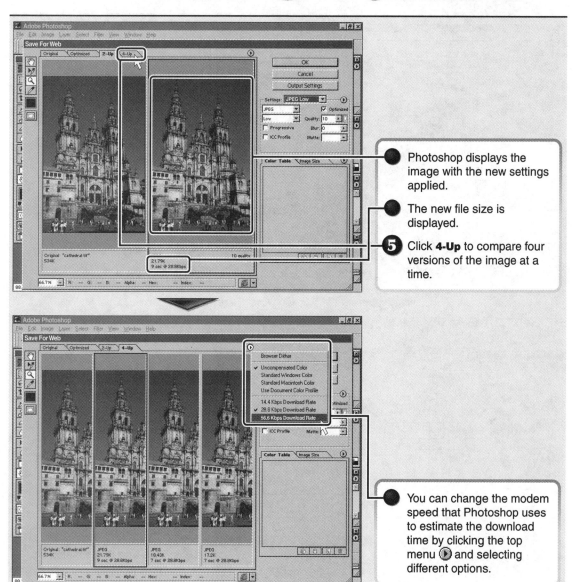

Photoshop displays the image with the new settings applied.

The new file size is displayed.

5 Click **4-Up** to compare four versions of the image at a time.

You can change the modem speed that Photoshop uses to estimate the download time by clicking the top menu ⊙ and selecting different options.

223

You can print your Photoshop images in color using color inkjet and dye-sublimation printers.

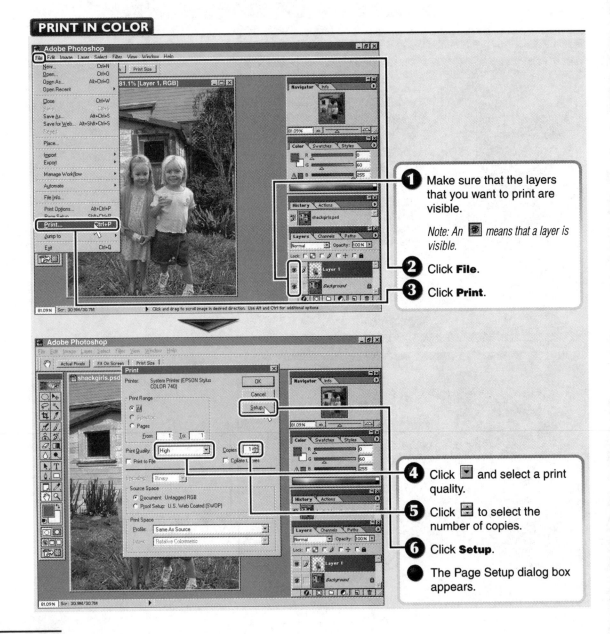

1 Make sure that the layers that you want to print are visible.

Note: An 👁 *means that a layer is visible.*

2 Click **File**.

3 Click **Print**.

4 Click 🔽 and select a print quality.

5 Click 🔼 to select the number of copies.

6 Click **Setup**.

● The Page Setup dialog box appears.

in an *instant*

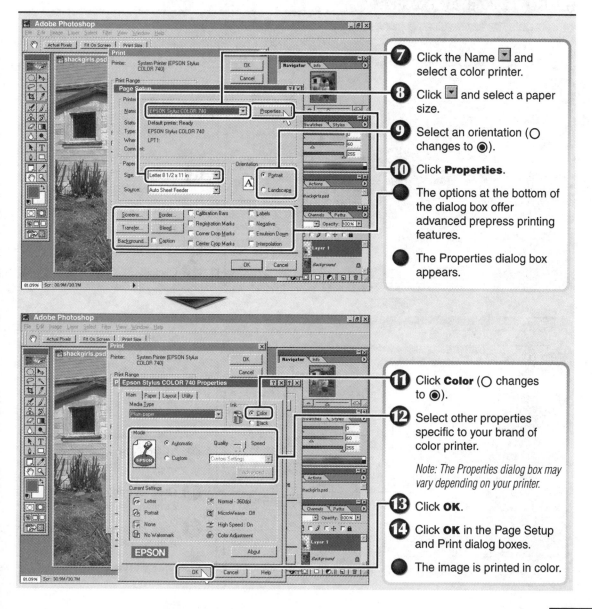

7 Click the Name ▼ and select a color printer.

8 Click ▼ and select a paper size.

9 Select an orientation (○ changes to ◉).

10 Click **Properties**.

● The options at the bottom of the dialog box offer advanced prepress printing features.

● The Properties dialog box appears.

11 Click **Color** (○ changes to ◉).

12 Select other properties specific to your brand of color printer.

Note: The Properties dialog box may vary depending on your printer.

13 Click **OK**.

14 Click **OK** in the Page Setup and Print dialog boxes.

● The image is printed in color.

PRINT IN BLACK AND WHITE

You can print in black and white on a laser printer or on a color printer set to black and white.

PRINT IN BLACK AND WHITE

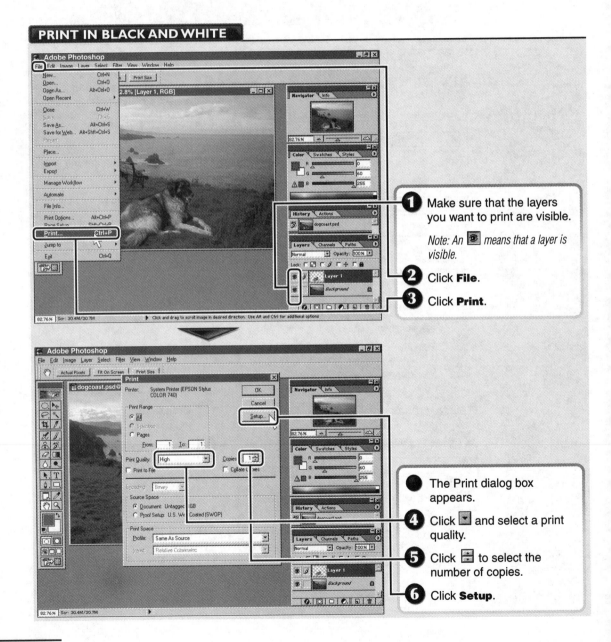

1 Make sure that the layers you want to print are visible.

Note: An ⬛ means that a layer is visible.

2 Click **File**.

3 Click **Print**.

■ The Print dialog box appears.

4 Click ⬛ and select a print quality.

5 Click ⬛ to select the number of copies.

6 Click **Setup**.

in an *instant*

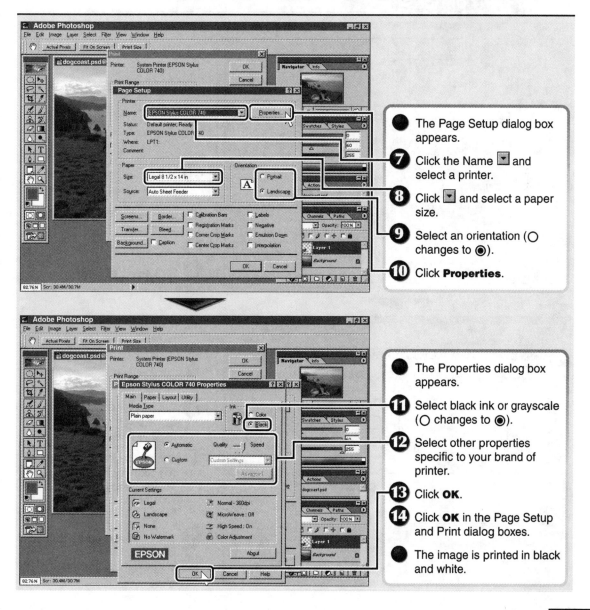

The Page Setup dialog box appears.

7 Click the Name ▾ and select a printer.

8 Click ▾ and select a paper size.

9 Select an orientation (○ changes to ◉).

10 Click **Properties**.

The Properties dialog box appears.

11 Select black ink or grayscale (○ changes to ◉).

12 Select other properties specific to your brand of printer.

13 Click **OK**.

14 Click **OK** in the Page Setup and Print dialog boxes.

The image is printed in black and white.

ADJUST PRINT OPTIONS

Photoshop lets you adjust the size and positioning
of your printed image in the Print Options dialog
box.

ADJUST PRINT OPTIONS

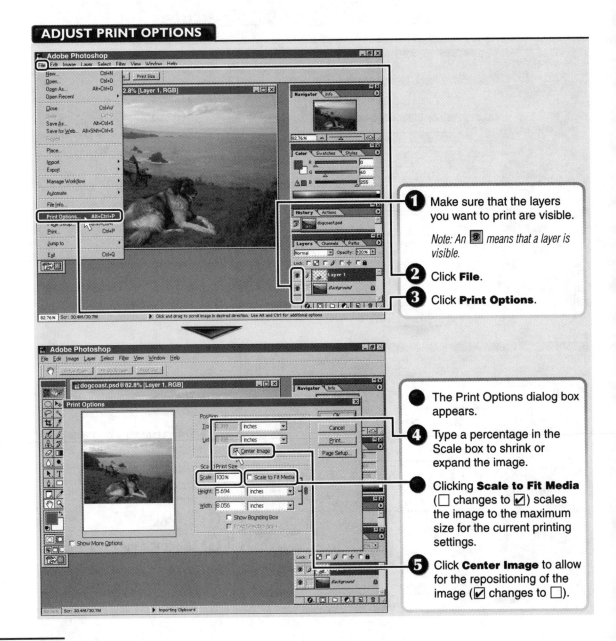

1 Make sure that the layers
you want to print are visible.

*Note: An 👁 means that a layer is
visible.*

2 Click **File**.

3 Click **Print Options**.

● The Print Options dialog box
appears.

4 Type a percentage in the
Scale box to shrink or
expand the image.

● Clicking **Scale to Fit Media**
(☐ changes to ☑) scales
the image to the maximum
size for the current printing
settings.

5 Click **Center Image** to allow
for the repositioning of the
image (☑ changes to ☐).

in an *instant*

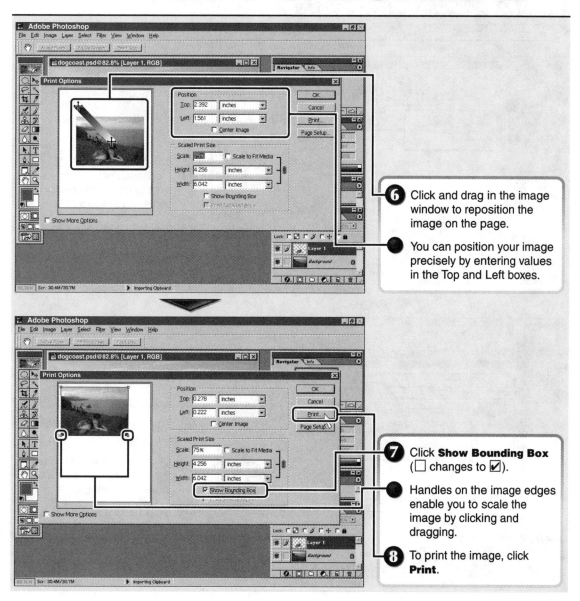

6 Click and drag in the image window to reposition the image on the page.

You can position your image precisely by entering values in the Top and Left boxes.

7 Click **Show Bounding Box** (☐ changes to ☑).

Handles on the image edges enable you to scale the image by clicking and dragging.

8 To print the image, click **Print**.

CREATE AND PRINT A CONTACT SHEET

Contact sheets are made up of thumbnail images and are useful for keeping a visual record of your full-size images. Photoshop can automatically create a contact sheet for you that you can print.

CREATE AND PRINT A CONTACT SHEET

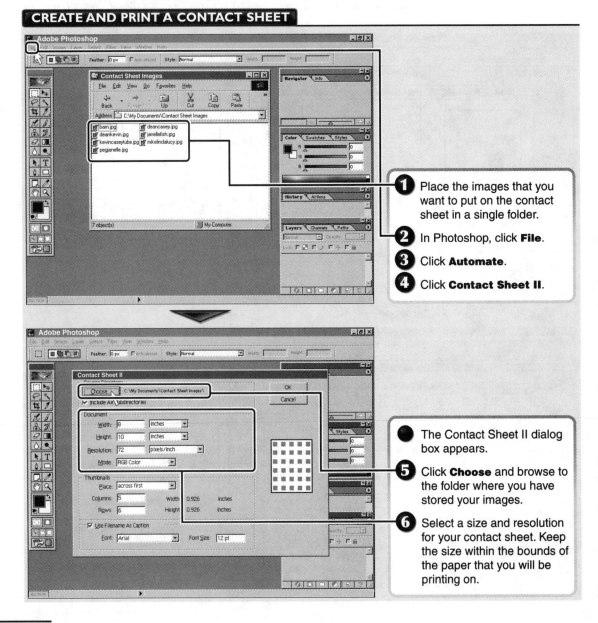

1. Place the images that you want to put on the contact sheet in a single folder.

2. In Photoshop, click **File**.

3. Click **Automate**.

4. Click **Contact Sheet II**.

● The Contact Sheet II dialog box appears.

5. Click **Choose** and browse to the folder where you have stored your images.

6. Select a size and resolution for your contact sheet. Keep the size within the bounds of the paper that you will be printing on.

in an *instant*

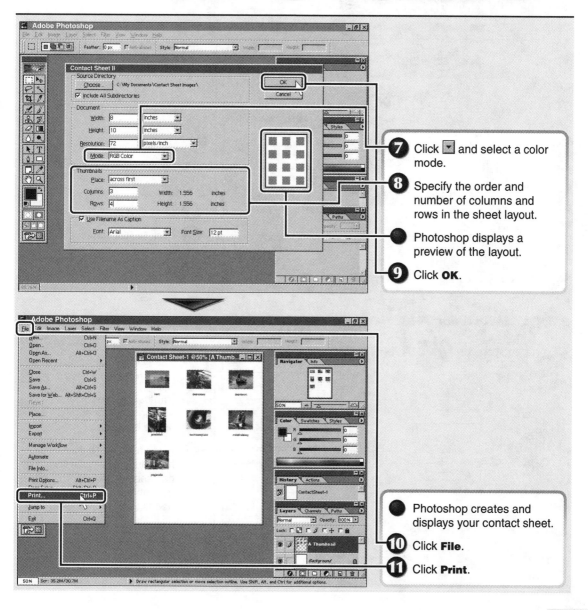

7 Click ▾ and select a color mode.

8 Specify the order and number of columns and rows in the sheet layout.

● Photoshop displays a preview of the layout.

9 Click **OK**.

● Photoshop creates and displays your contact sheet.

10 Click **File**.

11 Click **Print**.

ALLOCATE SCRATCH DISK SPACE

You can give Photoshop virtual memory, known as *scratch disk space*, from your hard drive to use when it runs out of RAM (random access memory). This enables you to open more files at once.

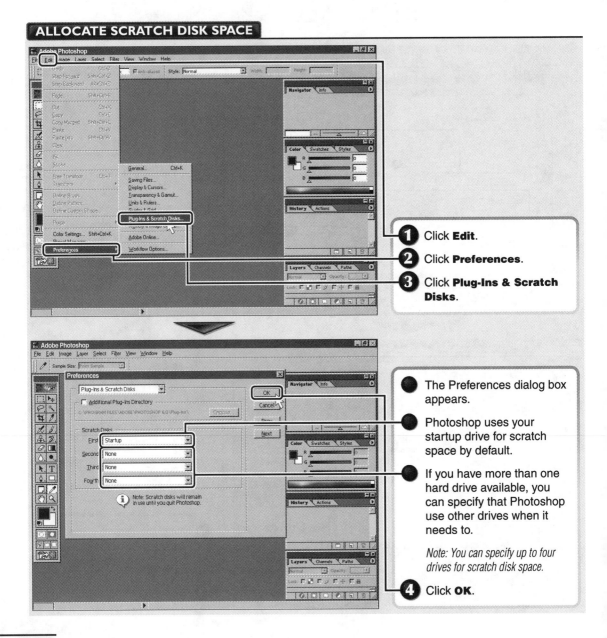

1 Click **Edit**.

2 Click **Preferences**.

3 Click **Plug-Ins & Scratch Disks**.

● The Preferences dialog box appears.

● Photoshop uses your startup drive for scratch space by default.

● If you have more than one hard drive available, you can specify that Photoshop use other drives when it needs to.

Note: You can specify up to four drives for scratch disk space.

4 Click **OK**.

in an *instant*

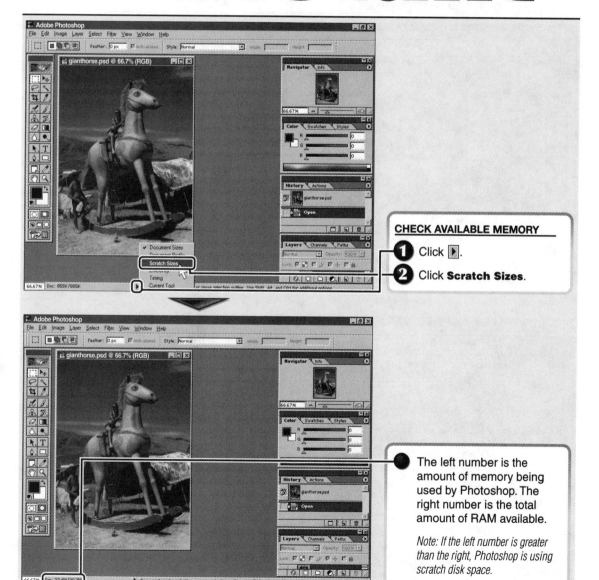

CHECK AVAILABLE MEMORY

1 Click ▶.

2 Click **Scratch Sizes**.

● The left number is the amount of memory being used by Photoshop. The right number is the total amount of RAM available.

Note: If the left number is greater than the right, Photoshop is using scratch disk space.

USING THE PURGE COMMAND

You can tell Photoshop to free up its History memory so that it can be used for other purposes. This can boost Photoshop's speed.

USING THE PURGE COMMAND

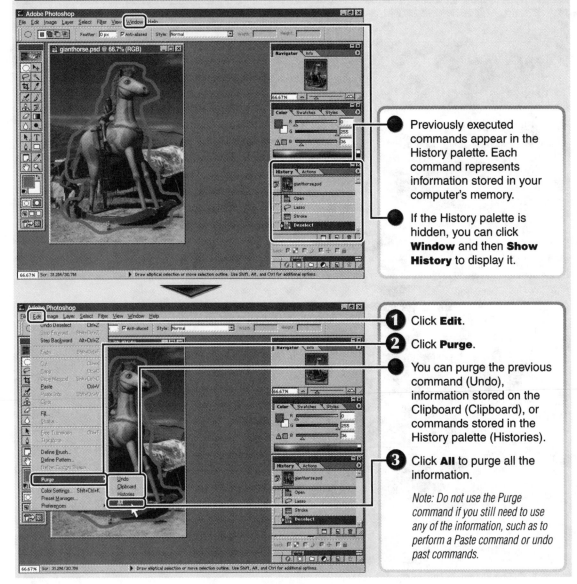

Previously executed commands appear in the History palette. Each command represents information stored in your computer's memory.

If the History palette is hidden, you can click **Window** and then **Show History** to display it.

1 Click **Edit**.

2 Click **Purge**.

You can purge the previous command (Undo), information stored on the Clipboard (Clipboard), or commands stored in the History palette (Histories).

3 Click **All** to purge all the information.

Note: Do not use the Purge command if you still need to use any of the information, such as to perform a Paste command or undo past commands.

in an *instant*

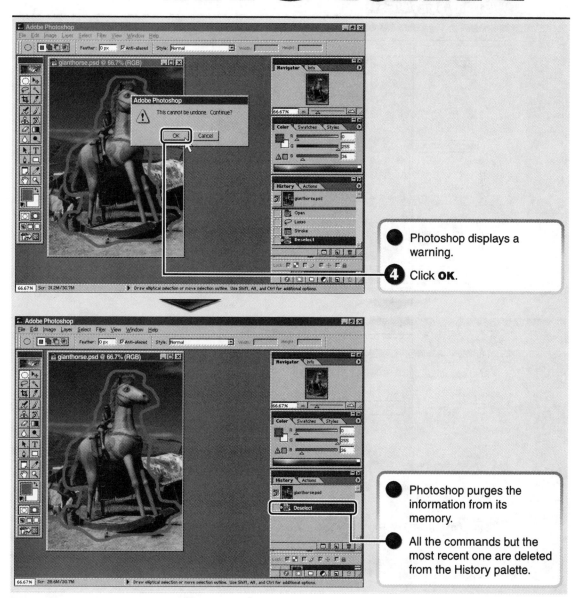

Photoshop displays a warning.

4 Click **OK**.

Photoshop purges the information from its memory.

All the commands but the most recent one are deleted from the History palette.

ADJUST HISTORY SETTINGS

You can control the amount of information stored in the History palette. This enables you to keep that information from taking up too much memory and slowing down Photoshop.

ADJUST HISTORY SETTINGS

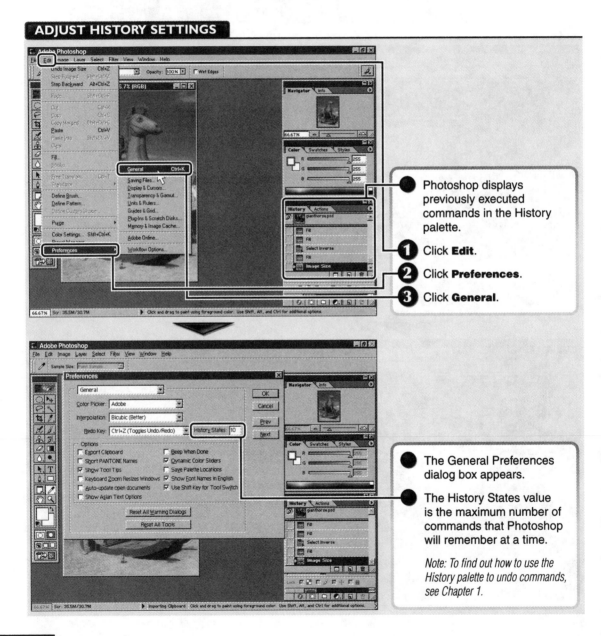

Photoshop displays previously executed commands in the History palette.

1 Click **Edit**.

2 Click **Preferences**.

3 Click **General**.

The General Preferences dialog box appears.

The History States value is the maximum number of commands that Photoshop will remember at a time.

Note: To find out how to use the History palette to undo commands, see Chapter 1.

in an *instant*

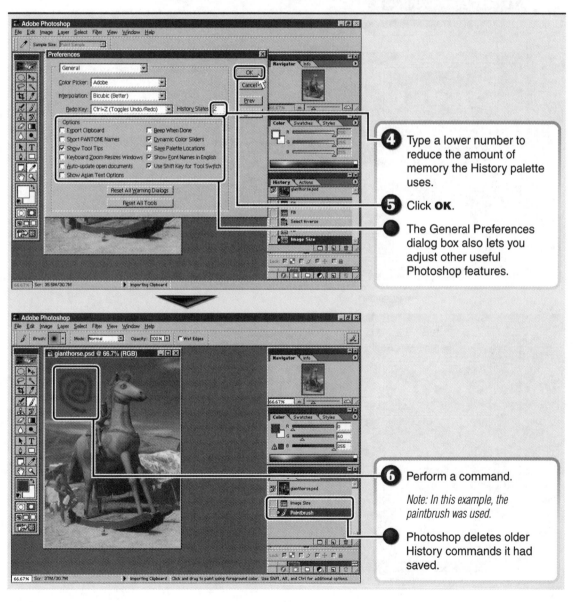

4 Type a lower number to reduce the amount of memory the History palette uses.

5 Click **OK**.

The General Preferences dialog box also lets you adjust other useful Photoshop features.

6 Perform a command.

Note: In this example, the paintbrush was used.

Photoshop deletes older History commands it had saved.

CREATE SLICED IMAGES

You can divide a large image that you want to display on the Web into smaller rectangular sections called *slices*. The different slices of an image can then be optimized independently of one another for faster download.

CREATE SLICED IMAGES

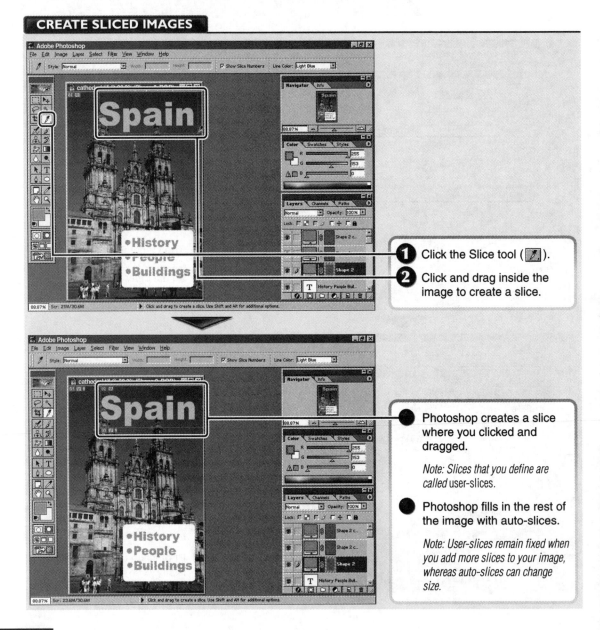

1 Click the Slice tool ( ).

2 Click and drag inside the image to create a slice.

Photoshop creates a slice where you clicked and dragged.

Note: Slices that you define are called user-slices.

Photoshop fills in the rest of the image with auto-slices.

Note: User-slices remain fixed when you add more slices to your image, whereas auto-slices can change size.

in an *instant*

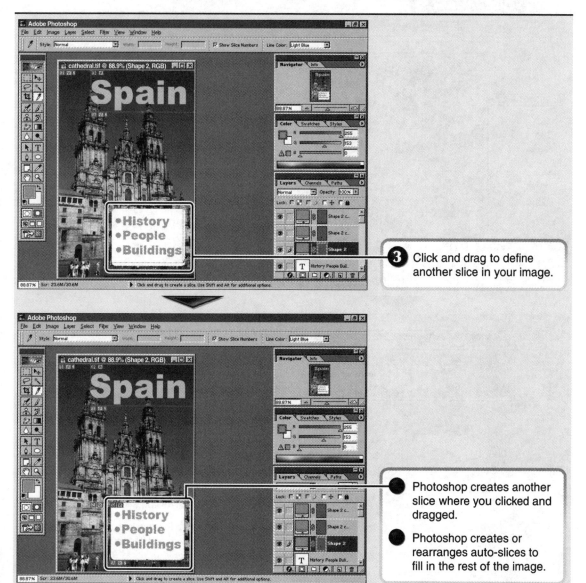

3 Click and drag to define another slice in your image.

● Photoshop creates another slice where you clicked and dragged.

● Photoshop creates or rearranges auto-slices to fill in the rest of the image.

SAVE SLICED IMAGES

You can save an image that has been partitioned using the Slice tool. Photoshop saves the slices as different images and also saves an HTML file that organizes the slices on a Web page. Slices enable you to save some parts of an image as GIF and others as JPEG. This can result in an overall image that has a smaller file size.

SAVE SLICED IMAGES

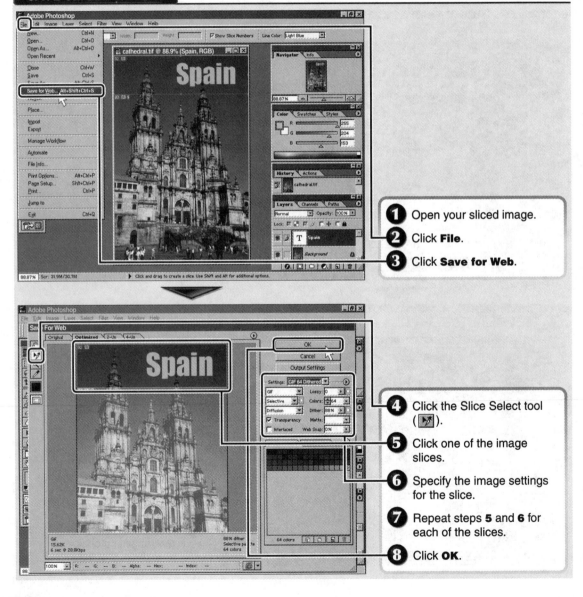

1. Open your sliced image.

2. Click **File**.

3. Click **Save for Web**.

4. Click the Slice Select tool ().

5. Click one of the image slices.

6. Specify the image settings for the slice.

7. Repeat steps **5** and **6** for each of the slices.

8. Click **OK**.

in an *instant*

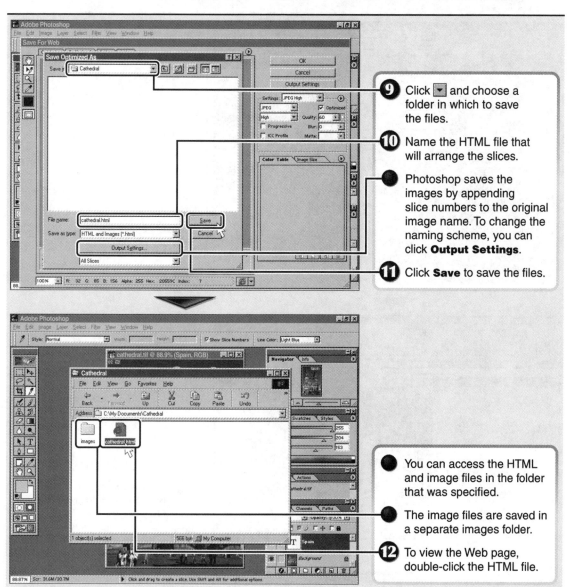

9 Click ▼ and choose a folder in which to save the files.

10 Name the HTML file that will arrange the slices.

● Photoshop saves the images by appending slice numbers to the original image name. To change the naming scheme, you can click **Output Settings**.

11 Click **Save** to save the files.

● You can access the HTML and image files in the folder that was specified.

● The image files are saved in a separate images folder.

12 To view the Web page, double-click the HTML file.

GET HELP

Photoshop comes with extensive documentation
that includes tips, suggestions, and ways to make
your editing tasks easier in case you ever need help.

GET HELP

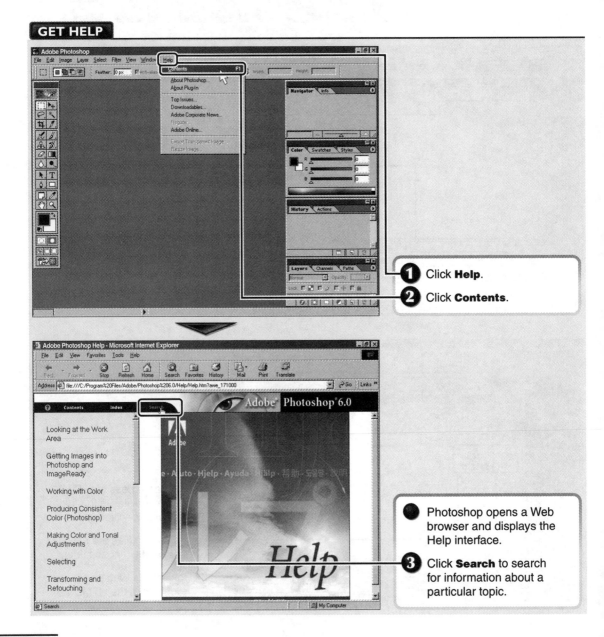

① Click **Help**.

② Click **Contents**.

● Photoshop opens a Web
browser and displays the
Help interface.

③ Click **Search** to search
for information about a
particular topic.

in an *instant*

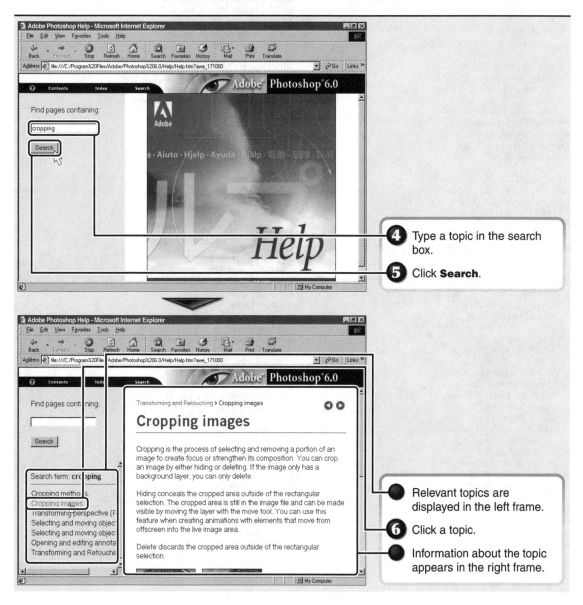

4 Type a topic in the search box.

5 Click **Search**.

● Relevant topics are displayed in the left frame.

6 Click a topic.

● Information about the topic appears in the right frame.

INDEX

INDEX

INDEX

INDEX

New from the Award-Winning Visual™ Series

in an *instant*

Fast
   Focused
      Visual
— and a great value!

- Zeroes in on the core tools and tasks of each application

- Features hundreds of large, super-crisp screenshots

- Straight-to-the-point explanations get you up and running — instantly

Other Visual Series That Help You
Read Less - Learn More™

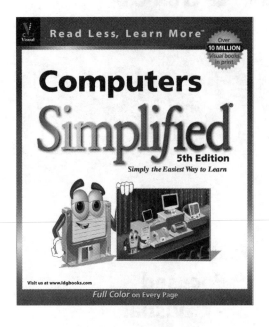

Simplified®

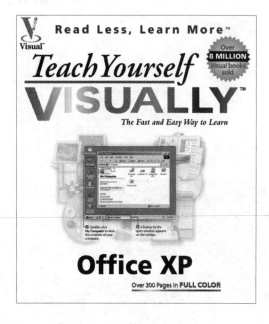

Teach Yourself VISUALLY™

Master VISUALLY™

Visual Blueprint

Available wherever books are sold